SOULWORK

SOULWORK

Clearing the Mind,

Opening the Heart,

Replenishing the Spirit

BettyClare Moffatt

Foreword by Sue Patton Thoele

WILDCAT CANYON PRESS • BERKELEY, CALIFORNIA

NEW WORLD LIBRARY • NOVATO, CALIFORNIA

Co-published by:

EDITORIAL OFFICE
Wildcat Canyon Press
PO Box 1974, #272
Berkeley, CA 94701

DISTRIBUTION OFFICE
New World Library
14 Pamaron Way
Novato, CA 94949

Cover Design: Sharon Smith Design
Cover Art: Wendy Schwartz
Interior Design and Production: Lory Poulson

Library of Congress Cataloging-in-Publication Data

Moffatt, BettyClare.
  Soulwork : clearing the mind, opening the heart, and replenishing the spirit / BettyClare Moffatt.
        p.   cm.
    Includes bibliographical references.
    ISBN 1-885171-01-3 (pbk.)
    1. Spiritual Life.   2. Moffatt, BettyClare.   I. Title.
BL624. M634 1994   94-15339
291.4'48—dc20   CIP

First printing September 1994
ISBN 1-885171-01-3
Distributed to the trade by Publishers Group West
10 9 8 7 6 5 4

For my mother,

my grandmothers,

my daughters-in-law,

my granddaughters and

all my women friends

and colleagues,

Soulworkers all,

I dedicate this book in

love, gratitude and joy.

Contents

Replenishing the Spirit

Foreword

Reading *Soulwork* is like sitting down to a tea party with a good and trusted friend. There you are with a steaming pot of tea and a plate of cookies on a sunny table, savoring an intimate, heartfelt conversation. Ms. Moffatt's warm and insightful words, down-to-earth wisdom, and delightful sense of humor encourage us, makes us feel loved and understood. Most of all, she lets us know that we are not alone.

Even though we've never met, after reading *Soulwork* I feel that I know BettyClare Moffatt and, more importantly, that she knows me. Her stories, struggles, and victories touched my heart. As with many of us, her life runs the gamut from laughter to tears and from tragedy to triumph, yet one of her main messages, and the one with the most resonance for my heart, is that it is possible to entertain joy in our lives no matter what the circumstances. Her steadfast belief that joy can permeate even our deepest darkness and can be overwhelmingly present during very simple acts, such as seeing a familiar tree with new eyes, encourages me to live, laugh, and love more fully—more joyfully. I think it will do the same for you.

In this wonderfully exciting—and often frustrating—time in which we are privileged to live, when feminine energy is being reawakened on our planet and reclaimed by many of us, Ms. Moffatt wears her well-earned wisdom in a jaunty and irreverent but nonetheless sacred style. It's fun to read how she has earned her merit badges over her fifty or so years. As readers, we identify with her experiences and learn practical ways of healing and opening ourselves to joy.

When I wrote *The Courage to Be Yourself*, *The Woman's Book of Courage*, and *The Woman's Book of Confidence,* my main goals were to help women know that they are not alone and to create a container in which we can expand our ability to love, accept, and trust ourselves. Stepping out of isolation and reaching out to give and receive support and wisdom from others empowers us and, in turn, revitalizes our personal lives, our families, businesses, governments, and our world in general. But first, we need to tend to ourselves. BettyClare Moffatt's *Soulwork* helps us with this all-important task.

Ms. Moffatt obviously loves being a woman. Her essays skillfully guide us, as we journey through our own crucibles of change, and gently teach us how to "clean up our inner attics" and keep the "worry wolf" from huffing and puffing his way into our lives. She inspires us with stories of angels and gives us hope that we may become, with the help of Grandmother Moon, grandmothers of courage, wisdom, and vision. She encourages us to curl up with our own personal memories and ruminations, our own inner trusted and true friend.

BettyClare Moffatt believes in herself, and her much-needed book provides encouragement for helping us believe in ourselves as well. If she can do it—regardless of what happens to cross her path—so can we!

Sue Patton Thoele
Boulder, Colorado

What Is Soulwork?

Soulwork is lifework.

Practicing Soulwork requires working through external layers of the personality in order to access the rich wisdom of the inner self. Through the processes of clearing the mind, opening the heart, and replenishing the spirit, we learn to embrace all of life, the world, nature, the universe, God, self, and others. Each life lesson we experience is a valuable step along the way. From the space of Soulwork, we can move into inner peace and harmony. Even the dark lessons of life are not to be missed. They contain valuable insights, increased understanding and compassion, and provide opportunities for wisdom and unconditional love.

Soulwork is not about fixing yourself or others or improving yourself or others or judging yourself or others. When you practice Soulwork, you choose to move through the world as a spiritual being encased in a human body, rather than a human being asking to be saved by outside forces or authorities.

The soul is your interior fulcrum, your balance point within, your point of focus, your entrance to the divine. You practice Soulwork by deep interior reflection, contemplation, and meditation—and by serving the world around you in an active, loving way according to your unfolding gifts. You practice Soulwork by living your life with integrity.

Soulwork helps you to experience your wholeness. It is all that you are, in both your humanness and in your spiritual life. It is not about fixing or improving or getting. It is about flowing and acknowledging and forgiving and allowing.

Soulwork is living with conscious grace and wisdom, whatever your circumstances, and using all that you are—body, mind, emotion, and spirit—in your ever-changing, individual dance of life.

I write what I most need to know. I live what I most need to write. And so I offer you *Soulwork*, from one heart to another. Will it touch you? Will it make a difference in your life, to have a friend to journey with, for a little while, through the avenues of life? Let me know of your own Soulwork—as I have shared mine with you. We have much to offer each other, dear friend.

BettyClare Moffatt
Fort Worth, Texas
April 1994

Clearing
the
Mind

WHEN YOU ARE FOCUSED

AND CLEAR, YOUR WORLD

AND YOUR TASKS IN IT WILL

FLOW FORWARD OF THEIR

OWN ACCORD

Throwing Stones

At a time in my life when despair seemed the order of the day and my teeth ground in frustration at every passing sling and arrow, I talked to a friend of mine who had weathered, with grace and courage, some of the same challenges that I was going through. I asked her what to do.

"Throw stones," she advised me.

"What?"

"It's an exercise, a ritual, an exorcism if you will," she said. Since my friend is practical, tough, and clearheaded, I swallowed my skepticism and asked for details.

"It's called the resentment exercise," she explained, "and I'll share it with you, but you must promise to do all the steps involved. Just thinking about it isn't enough."

"Why?" I asked again.

"Because the mind needs concrete evidence to rearrange its patterns, and the emotions need motion in order to do the same."

I dutifully promised.

It was like a recipe. It went like this:

Write down on a piece of paper all—all!—the frustrations and resentments you are filled with, past and present, trivial or catastrophic.

"*All?*" I inquired again in disbelief.

"Well," she said, "the first time I did this exercise, I couldn't bear to write down my feelings about my father's stroke, my mother's violent, uncontrollable Alzheimer's, or the book project that fell through after months of work." (She is a writer too.) "Write down most of your resentments," she said. "You can tackle the major issues later, in a month or two, after you lighten the load."

It definitely needed lightening. But in my curious, stubborn fashion, my essential nature got the better of me, and I included everything on my list. I counted twenty-one hurts, angers, fears. How could anyone hold twenty-one resentments over the years? I told you I included everything.

"Number the resentments," advised my friend, "and then go to the store and buy a marking pen."

I did as I was told.

"Now," she said, "gather stones."

"What?"

"Gather stones. Go out to the country or a park and gather stones." I didn't need to ask how many.

4

"Yes," she affirmed. "One stone for each numbered resentment on your list. Mark each stone with a corresponding number. Then," she said, "you'll be ready. You'll be ready to throw your stones."

The day was stormy when I began to gather my stones, my list and marking pen clutched in my hand. I gathered them by color, weight, size, configuration. Not unlike, I reflected, the individual resentments on my list. I felt both foolish and mysterious. I was an ancient priestess gathering gifts to assuage the fates. The situation portended good.

Here was a rock for heartbreak — sharp and jagged with gray-blue veins running through it. Here was a heavy, slimy, misshapen stone. I knew what number I would write on it. Here were small stones of triviality. Here were stones of dark and deep. I gathered them all, twenty-one stones, each one discrete and different, each one a problem unresolved, each one an emotional universe.

I sat on the curb above the park, there where the sere and wintry grass hugged a ravine full of brush. I sorted my stones. I marked my stones, white ink on dark rock. I consulted my list. I looked everywhere around me. There was no one watching. Only me and my stones.

Then, slowly, carefully, ceremoniously, I began to throw

my stones into the ravine, whispering their messages after them as they skidded down the hill. When I was finished, even the wind was still. There was only the echo of my voice on the air and the sound of my breath, gritty as gravel, in my throat. I tore up the written list and scattered its strips into the ravine as well.

"No more," I said. "Done." I might have said more. But I noticed then that the gravel in my throat was gone. As was the heaviness in my gut. As was the pain in my right side that had plagued me with its insistent, incessant throbbing. As was the stone that had heretofore pierced my heart. I was lighter. I was clear. I was empty.

I called my friend. I told her about throwing stones. "I may have to repeat the experience in a few months," I told her. "There may be more."

"Of course," she said. "There's bound to be more." Her mother had just died, without recognizing the face of the daughter who had cared for her.

I offered to come to her area of the country to be with her. "We could," I ventured, "throw stones together."

She began to cry. "Hurry," she said to me. "Bring stones. Bring lots and lots of stones."

An Apple Woman

According to a magazine article I just read, middle-aged, overweight women come in two categories. They are classified as pear women or apple women. I never knew that. I thought I was unique.

Oh, I knew of course that I was an apple woman. Ever since I gave up self-hatred for Lent, I have noticed who I am without dismay. A bout of yearning hits me every now and then, but since I eat lightly (low fat, high fiber, no meat, no alcohol), since I exercise (walking, yoga, dance), since I am by nature short, near the earth, built for stamina, grounded, since the days of running marathons are over and my own unique combination of aging, genetics, occupation, and a pesky endocrine system have served to shape me just so, since I know all these things, I know, of course, that I am an apple woman.

This I regard as more fortunate than most do. For I love apples. They are shiny and round and radiate health (and, I like to think, goodwill) on the outside. They keep the doctor away. Inside, oh inside, apples are bursting with firm flesh and densely packed juices. They are both tart and sweet. Crisp, crunchy, packed with vitamins. They satisfy. They nourish. They sustain.

So it is with me.

Perhaps someday, when labels and classifications fall by the wayside, when emaciation signifies death instead of beauty, the world will remember apple women. Then we will come into our own.

I'm starting now. For I am an apple woman.

The Forgiveness Boat

This is the hardest thing to write about and the hardest thing to live. Because I'll bet you a million dollars that no one—no one!—on this planet has mastered forgiveness. We are still discovering and uncovering levels and layers of resistance to total, complete, unconditional forgiveness. I'll bet you anything! One path of mastery tells us that "forgiveness is our only function." In other words, this is what we're here for, and, in each life lesson we encounter, there's a chance, an opportunity, a need, for forgiveness.

Don't get me wrong. I don't go about on my hands and knees, gnawing at the past like a dog with a bone, trying to get past old stuck places in my heart and mind. Actually, sometimes I do. When I am stuck, I find myself pounding on the door of my good with fierce and bloody hands. That's when I try to go past where I am now and into the next step of my life. At those times, I'll take forgiveness, I'll give forgiveness, I'll function as forgiveness.

Anything to get this damn stubborn boat off the shore, into the water, and over to the other side. The boat is a good analogy. I like it. I think I'll keep it. Because if I have a forgiveness boat, I can put all the things that don't work in my life into it, all the niggling, hateful things that just do not cooperate with me—yes, those emotions!—those old ragged feelings, those old ruts in the mind that make a circle. If I have a forgiveness boat, I can put into it not only what I no longer want to deal with—because I'm tired of all this, and let's get on with it!— but I can also put into the boat all the techniques and processes I've learned over the years.

I love techniques, processes, mind exercises, energy games. Anything to keep the energy moving, so that I can get unstuck and heave that boat out onto the lake of soul. Mixed metaphors, but you get what I mean. I would put the techniques for clearing and cleansing and healing and yes, of course, for forgiving into the boat. I'd pack them in with the problems and emotions that just won't let go of me, and I would let them fight it out.

But where does that leave me? On the shore, waiting for another boat? Watching the one on the lake sink because of its warring factions? Not likely. I guess I'll have to get into the boat myself and row, row, row my forgiveness boat as I mediate between the problems and the resolutions.

You probably know all about forgiveness exercises. They're like resentment exercises or anger exercises or guilt exercises (it's almost always false guilt, for leaving undone the things we ought to have done, as the old prayer goes) or fear exercises (fear is only False Evidence Appearing Real). All of them *do* work.

You can write your feelings out in a journal and change them to another feeling with affirmations, or scream out your feelings in the shower, or pound a pillow, or take a walk, or talk to a friend, lover, spouse, clergy, or professional helper of any kind you choose. You can have a startling array of body work done to you and with you to get the feelings moving. You can chant and you can sing and you can dance. You can throw stones. You can write all your feelings down on pieces of paper and then burn them or bury them or flush them down the toilet. Or you can think up some original, unique way of moving the energy inherent in the resentment, anger, guilt, or fear. (I don't count grief. Grief is a long process that can't be rushed or covered over or ignored. Sometimes it must just be endured until time itself heals or mitigates the wounds.)

So there are lots of things you can do to change the energy you don't want to the energy you do want. And they're all good techniques, processes, exercises. But they are not the boat. And neither are you.

There is an ancient meditation that begins: "I have a body, but I am not my body. I have a mind, but I am not my mind. I have emotions, but I am not my emotions." Then it goes on to tell us that we are more than the problems and more than the processes, that we are unchanging and eternal energy. That puts it all into perspective, doesn't it?

So when we put the problems and the processes into the forgiveness boat and send it off across the deep, unconscious waters of our souls and let it drift with the current or fight it out with the waves or even capsize and right itself and find its way, we can be apart from that, shading our eyes to watch the forgiveness boat go farther and farther and farther until it disappears over the horizon. And know that we are serene and calm and balanced and light. Know that we are eternal and unchanging and renewing spirit. And wave the forgiveness boat onward, with all its fragile freight.

Pray it onward. Release it. Give it up. Let it go. Allow. Let it be.

The Turning Point

There comes a time in the life of each of us when certain crucial choices must be made. There comes a time when all our ways of dealing with the problems of the world, the problems of others, and the problems within us, will no longer work. All the doors formerly open to us in our constantly busy, accustomed way of dealing with the world slam shut!

There is an impasse, a point beyond which we cannot go, and all the beating of fists and head upon the cold closed entryway will not admit us to the safe place where we want to be. All doors seem locked. Obstacles and obstructions arise to exhaust the outer mind and all the possible courses of action it can conceive. We ourselves, by an immense effort of will, and with gritted teeth, can only go haltingly forward to perform daily duties. Nothing seems to work.

This condition is, in reality, a turning point. When we can no longer go on in our accustomed way, the machinery within us can (and often does) shudder to a halt.

What do we choose to do at that halting place? Do we choose consciously at all? Or is it a holy spark within that ignites us toward another higher way of being in the world? Do we choose, or are we chosen?

Sometimes it seems as though we are turned in new directions by our own conscious reasoning mind, which, wanting so much for us to succeed at this business of living, is willing to risk a possible "breakdown" in order to accomplish a "breakthrough" into consciousness. Sometimes we are turned in unaccustomed directions by a force that seems not of us, a gentle, subtle force that moves us against our conscious will into a new pattern.

This force for good is an instinctive thing. It is as if we are light reflectors, and, in order to continue absorbing the energy from the sun and to pass along that energy to others, we must be turned to a new angle of vision—in order to absorb and capture the sunlight that is waiting to make us whole and new. The soul within each of us responds to the "solar energy" all around us when we turn or are turned to that sunlight. As a flower turns toward the sun in order to grow, so we turn toward that warm flowing energy within, that force for good in the universe, which can lead us away from closed doors, into a garden of peace and fulfillment.

To recognize the process and allow this power to take over in our lives is the first great step toward spiritual freedom. To relinquish the frantic control of self and others to this infinite intelligence restores rather than repudiates our whole self.

To cease our fighting, our struggle, our strain, our pain, to become still, is a major step in turning toward our good. We do it because we must, because we truly have no other choice if we are to go on.

This process is not a "giving up," it is a "letting go." For to get what we most desire as our highest good in life, we must let go of all we do not want. To *get*, *let*! Then it is that the words we have whispered in prayer through anguished nights and days take over with new life, new meaning.

"God is in charge. God is meeting the need now." Sometimes these are the only words we need in order to recognize what is happening, in order to trust that whatever is happening within can only be for our good.

Trust! "Trusting, trusting, trusting, I am trusting You now," can, by its prayerful affirmation, bring into our lives all the rich treasures that God has "in trust" for us.

Our task is to believe, to trust, to create, to do whatever is at hand to do in the present moment. And to let the future be.

Our task is to affirm our own energy, our own God-identity, to use the gifts of the heart, the hands, and the spirit within, in the best way we know at the present moment.

Then comes the flow of light into our lives, as we "let go and let God," as we turn toward God, who is always and forever turned toward us.

The Whole Enchilada

My mother went to a new doctor, endured new tests, and then saw a new neurologist. The news was cautiously positive. My sister, my mother and I rejoiced. We decided to celebrate. We went to our favorite Mexican restaurant. We were giddy with relief.

There is a custom I have, taught to me long ago as I grew up in the middle of the Depression. No, it's not "eat everything on your plate because the children in China are starving." When I was growing up, restaurant meals were rare, reserved for birthdays or special celebrations, and not an everyday occurrence. My custom is to carefully and deliberately eat only half of my food at a restaurant meal and take the other half home for another day. Waste not, want not. This frugality helps both my waistline and my pocketbook. So when I go out to eat Mexican food, I eat only one or two bites of my vegetarian enchiladas and half my beans and rice and thriftily carry the rest home. My sister is both slender and financially secure, but she too follows the family habit, as does my mother, who can eat only a little at a time. So we ate and laughed and talked and carried three large containers of festive leftovers out of the restaurant.

After helping my mother into her house, my sister and I talked in the car, enjoying a few blessed moments alone without the rest of the family. We are opposites in every way, shape, and form. Our mother is our common bond and common concern. But we opened up to one another. We discussed fears and old resentments. We hugged and settled things. I felt as if a huge weight had lifted from me as I watched her car leave my driveway for its hour-and-a-half journey to her home.

I went inside, closed my door, and leaned against it in a sag of relief. Suddenly I was ravenously hungry. But my leftover enchiladas, tomorrow's dinner, were bouncing to my sister's house in the back of her car. My careful denial of my body's need to eat had been thwarted. I laughed again and again.

Sometimes you just have to feast. Sometimes you need to be greedy, not careful. Sometimes you have to savor each moment and each bite as life, glorious life, continues for your loved ones. Sometimes worry, about tomorrow's meal or tomorrow's money or tomorrow's responsibilities, is futile.

Sometimes there is enough for you to savor right now, instead of saving for a rainy day.

Sometimes you just have to eat the whole enchilada.

Next time I will.

Risk, Character, and Failure

I write these Soulwork passages to understand and heal myself, as much as for any other reason. An incident, a story, a phone call, the cry of a friend, any or all will trigger just what I need to know myself for resolution. Or having once known, for remembering, for reconciliation with myself.

When the publishing company into which I had put all my energy, identity, mind, body, heart, and soul went under, I almost went under too. I had stretched myself, I had walked on water, I had prayed my way into and through these "Books to Serve the World," as my mission statement read. I had come to the cliff again and again. I had thrown myself forward in sheer trust.

"Teach me! Use me!" I had cried. I *was* this company, this mission, this dream.

And then, overextended and under-financed, I was hit by the huge wave of recession bearing down on the city where I lived and worked. It fell like a merciless tidal wave from the ocean a scant few blocks away. And seven years of work and prayer were gone.

"Don't take it personally," another publisher advised me. "Everyone in business goes through this sooner or later. Why, I've never known a millionaire yet who didn't have a bankruptcy under his belt."

But I was not a millionaire. I was not a bankrupt person. What I was, no matter what anyone said, was a failure. Worse, it was a failure of character, as well as money. I had made promises I could not keep. I had let other people's dreams die. I had failed to support staff, authors, the community. I had let everyone down. And I couldn't pay all my business bills. No matter what I did, cajoling heaven, asking for a sign from God, making promises I could not possibly keep, I was a failure. I had failed to keep all my agreements. Especially my ironclad agreements with myself. Like an old-fashioned knight in a fairy tale, my very honor was at stake.

People I respected and loved helped me to close the business, pay off everyone I possibly could, and return home. Once there, I shook like a leaf, convinced that I would be hauled off to debtors' prison in iron chains. Worse yet, other people needed me and expected more of me than I had left to give. I hit rock bottom inside myself. I could no longer serve the world. I could no longer help anyone else. I had risked everything and failed.

Finding my way back to self-respect, self-caring, and self-forgiveness was not easy. There was no blinding light on the road, no clearly defined turning point. While there may very well have been angels to guide me, I was oblivious of their presence. I only knew that I had to come to some sort of understanding with myself and make peace with the forces that I thought had destroyed my dreams.

I began an interior search and started to take apart all the ideas, beliefs, judgments, and assumptions I had made about myself over a lifetime. I prayed and meditated. I called on angelic beings to assist me, even though a forlorn part of myself doubted that they would ever hear. I wrote book after book that did not sell. I did what was at hand with family and with friends. Somehow I supported myself.

One day while walking the streets of my neighborhood, I noticed that spring had come again, after a long winter. Redbirds flashed through the pecan and magnolia trees and perched on honeysuckle and lavender bushes. The rosebud tree had bloomed. Families were out walking with their children and dogs.

A toddler zoomed across my line of vision. She was dressed in a yellow sunsuit, and she had on those high-top white Buster Brown training shoes that I remembered from my own childhood. She didn't take hesitant steps. No, she plowed right into passersby in her excitement to get to the flower beds in each yard. She would make a beeline from sidewalk to grass, fall, act surprised, tear up and pout for a moment, and then heave herself up on her hands and knees and go boldly forward. She would clutch at the grass as she fell, again and again, and look around bewildered for help. She looked at her fat knees which had buckled under her, surprised and indignant. Once she fell on gravel, her round bottom hitting the rocks with a thud and a splat. She cried then, surprised and angry at her means of locomotion letting her down.

Her father started to rush to her side. Her mother stopped him. "No! She's all right. She just has to learn. She'll pick herself up. See!"

Another neighbor, an elderly woman with a cane, recovering from a heart attack, had stopped to watch the little drama with me.

"I feel just like that child," she commented in her sweet, high voice. "I'm having to learn to walk all over again." She pointed at my foot. "And how is yours?"

Despite a sprain in my instep which had almost crippled me when I first returned home, I walked every day the sun shone, a little farther each time, although my foot often dragged and pulled a little on the way home.

"Oh, it's much better," I told her. "Almost healed."

The little girl toddled to her parents, triumphant, yellow dandelions clutched in her fist. They laughed and lifted her up. She wriggled out of her parents' arms.

"More!" she announced, and she made right for the wildflowers that sprinkled my yard. We all stood there, neighbors on a sunny afternoon, exchanging pleasantries, watching a child learn to walk, fall down, hit her bottom, scrape her knees, get up and walk again, all in pursuit of wildflowers.

"What will we do," her father chuckled, "when she starts kindergarten? There'll be no stopping her."

All risk is relative. Failure's just a word. As for character, mine is only bruised, not broken. And maybe, just maybe, character is getting up after falling down, again and again and again, while searching for wildflowers among the rocks. And never stopping until you find them. Even when you have to learn to walk all over again.

The Listening Soul

When you are honest with yourself, you will find out the truth about yourself. When you consistently enter the silence, with or without other techniques of meditation, you will come to a place (it is different for each of us and yet it is the same) where there is nothing.

Nothing at all.

I call it the Listening Soul.

Once you have quieted your body, established your breathing pattern, and surrounded yourself with light, pouring it through you from the crown of your head to the tip of your toes, grounding the light and yourself in the earth, carrying the light around your body to suffuse you in its protective arena, you do—nothing.

No mantras, no images, no visualizations, no supplications. If anything at all is said by you, it would be this, and only at the beginning of this quiet time:

"I am listening."

All other meditative techniques are just that, techniques, and are practiced to get us to the place where we can learn to listen.

Meditation of this sort is true contemplation. It is a still-ness within, a true hearing on interior levels. The mind may react strongly at first and refuse this assignment. Objects, feelings, and images may rush behind your eyelids. You may fidget, itch, scratch, yawn. A restless mind in a restless body.

Be still. Let the mind stuff, the illusions, the dream-scape, go. Be still.

For you are here to give back a portion of that time and attention given to you. A tithing of time, a tithing of self, back to the source of all that is good.

Words may float into your mind. Accept these words as right for you to hear. Or there may be no words at all after the initial chatter subsides.

There may be a subtle interior adjustment as you settle into peacefulness. There may be a sudden onrush of joy. You may find silent tears coursing down your cheeks. There may be a profound exquisite silence.

There may be nothing. There may be everything. It is all right.

In such quietness and serenity, turn within and listen. As you listen, you will come to that place of deep silence. Beyond that place is everything. Beyond that place you begin to fill up, to be light and to transmit that light, whether it be candle or bonfire, into the darkness all around you. You become the lighted lamp of your being. You become your own center of light.

You can illuminate any relationship, any situation, with this light. You can be so overflowing with light and love that you don't need to "get" all the time. You can be the giving, the flow. And you can be that flow consistently, as you become aware that all you give is given to yourself, all that you give comes back to you.

Be kind to yourself, be tender and forgiving as you begin this practice of listening to the soul. Let all that you have struggled for, strived for, wished for, hoped for, dreamed for, fought for, dissolve into that silence of your soul. It has its own agenda. And it is a loving one. Allow. Allow it to unfold. Just listen.

I Have No Doubt

I always knew what I wanted to do. I just didn't know how, during various decades of my life, I would do it. Life intervened while I was on the way to publication.

I remember a turning point in my life. My sons were rebellious teenagers, I had a full-time teaching job, and I was going to graduate school. (Thank God I will not pass that way again!)

I also was blessed, at that period in my overworked, chaotic life, by having a woman minister as a friend and my first spiritual teacher. Somehow I carved out enough time to take classes with her. She wasn't the only one to teach me meditation and universal laws and spiritual truths, but she was the dearest.

One day I went to her in tears. My family problems seemed insolvable. I was playing peacemaker in a family of angry, confused men. I kept warring factions at bay, even while I pleaded and interceded and drove myself and my children to counseling. I was balancing on a tightrope, my arms filled with troubles, inching gingerly across a chasm that loomed below me, afraid at any moment I might fall.

I poured all this out to my spiritual teacher. A poised and peaceful older woman, she listened in silence. She didn't offer to fix anything. She didn't suggest biblical platitudes, although she was a deeply religious woman. We sat in meditation for a few moments, until the air cleared and I was calmer.

Then she asked me one question. "What is your deepest dream?"

Startled, I looked at her. "Well, if only…and if this were changed…and if he would…" and I continued wearily with my original litany.

She shook her head, put her fingers to her lips. I subsided into silence again.

"What is your deepest dream? What would you do if you could do anything in the world, without the problems you now have?"

"But I can't have what I want because of…" I began again.

"No." She held up her hand for silence.

"Not for anyone else, not for others' dreams, not because of or in spite of. What is your deepest dream?"

And in a rush of words I told her. "My deepest dream is to write wise and loving books that touch the hearts of women everywhere. That make a difference in the world. That serve in some way. That are good, true, and beautiful."

We sat in silence again, while the words echoed in the room.

"But can I do it?" I ventured timidly. "I've always been a writer, but I haven't been able to do what I wanted to for years. Can I really do it?"

She smiled at me serenely. "I have no doubt," she said firmly and with an air of absolute finality.

"I have no doubt." I carried those words with me for years, as my life straightened out in unexpected and, to the casual eye, unbelievable and risky turns of fate. "I have no doubt."

Often during all those years, I did indeed have doubts. Sometimes it seemed that doubt lurked in a corner, and, if I turned my head, he would rush forward to devour me. Or at the very least deflect me from my course.

Then I would take deep breaths, and quiet myself, and become one-pointed, single-minded, focused. I would become an arrow flying to its target. I would become a bird soaring to its high and treasured nest.

Years later, when my first book was published, I gave her a copy. She asked me then to give a lecture to her spiritual classes. I even taught classes myself, for a while, in that church home. She had taught me well.

I continued to present my teacher with the books I had written, one by one as they were published, each time I revisited my hometown and her. I published other people's books as well for a number of years. I made a difference in the world.

The wheel has come full circle. I am back in the place where it all started, a five word question, a five word answer, a four word statement. Taped next to my computer is a note that bears the legend, "I have no doubt."

So I will ask you the question now: "What is your deepest dream?" I hear your answer, tumbling forth from that deep well of longing that lies in each of us. And then your question: "Can I really do it?"

"I have no doubt."

Dreaming in Categories

I dream in categories.

I use my dreams as healing tools. More than using them to program health, I often ask dream angels to just go ahead and heal whatever needs to be healed next, even if I do not know, in my waking life, exactly what the next thing is. This works well for me, although I often sleep much longer when I ask for help than when I try to do it all myself. I respect that time in which the logical, rational, figuring-it-out self can rest and let the highest and the best in me take over.

I dream in clusters. Sometimes it takes three days or a week or a month or more to wrestle with some unresolved plaint inside of me, some area of my emotional life that cries out for solution. For you never dream about what has already been solved, resolved, made whole. You dream about what you are developing, what you are healing, what you are going toward. You dream in color and in categories, yes, you dream in magic and in mysticism, you dream in hope and prayer. You dream in your own private language. You dream your self into being.

Sometimes dreams, like life, defy categories. Sometimes dreams not only heal your life, but also save your life.

Once, when my life had crumbled before me like a bad movie and I wandered, dazed and bereft, through my waking life, I dreamed such a dream.

I was drowning. I tried to get to the other side of a lake that was ringed round by mountains. I was on one shore, despairing and, I surmise, out of control because the car I was driving, my own in real life, plunged into the lake and tried to swim across it with me inside, frantically vying for control. But there was no bottom to the lake, no footing . So I began to drown, going down with the vehicle that had brought me to the very middle of the lake, where both shores were equidistant, both equally impossible, or so it seemed to me. The water filled the car and filled my mouth and nose as well. I prayed for rescue.

Then something happened. I saw a figure. It looked like a female winged Mercury, holding a silver transparent globe—the world itself—aloft. This figure came winging to me over the waters and reached down to take my hand and pull me out of the sinking vehicle, carrying me to the other shore. Mercury, the goddess of writing and of communication, leading me to another shore.

I woke up. I wrote down my dream. I trembled with its truth.

I knew then that I would be all right. That I would use my talents and my abilities to write my way out of this drowning crisis. That all that I could communicate, both in my writing and in my life, would rescue me.

We each choose private symbols that resonate with levels of meaning. Dreaming in categories or dreaming that one single, heartfelt, yearning dream, we dream in metaphor. We dream in symbol, in story and singing and prayer . We dream truth.

And sometimes, when we have lost our way, when we have left one shore and cannot find our way, in waking life, to the other side, when we are drowning, we dream of rescue.

And it always comes.

Interior Clean Up

There's a great technique that I often use when joy is covered and clouded over by too much stuff in my life. It's called the Interior Clean Up.

All you do is close your eyes and go into the attic of your mind and explore the dusty keepsakes and nightmares that have been stuffed into trunks and all the other dirty, old, worn-out, used-up furniture of your mind that is no longer serving you.

Go into the attic and clear out and throw out and give away everything you can find that needs to be discarded. You know the things I mean. Worn-out thought forms, old resentments, odd clumps of hatred, jealousies with holes in them, trunks full of buried feelings—everything that you no longer want, need, or desire. Do it easily, without too much huffing and puffing. And the first time or two, don't be too zealous in your Interior Clean Up. For you will certainly have to do this exercise more than once.

Now when you have discarded all that needs to be discarded in the attic of your mind, all that stuff that stands in the way of any joy or light coming in the attic windows, take the garbage bags and dispose of them. I put mine out at an imaginary curb. You can even bury them.

Use your mental ingenuity. Use your mental creativity. Use mental laughter too.

That's what a friend of mine did, when she sat down to do the Interior Clean Up. Lo and behold she discovered a large, bulky, shrouded object in the corner of her mental attic. She approached it with fear and trembling and whisked its moth-eaten blanket off. What do you think was hidden there? An old refrigerator, exactly like the one that stood in her parents' home throughout the forties and the fifties. She opened it. The little light came on inside. It was filled with moldy food and spoiled leftovers. Here were the food issues of my friend's childhood, now carried into adult life. Here were half-digested experiences. Here were half-gnawed bones.

"It was a liberating experience," she told me later, "to clean out my interior refrigerator. I even hauled the old refrigerator of my childhood out to a landfill and discarded it as well." She chuckled. "Sometimes an Interior Clean Up gives you food for thought."

I think I'll try her visualization.

What will you do with your clean, scrubbed, shining, empty attic room?

You begin to fill the empty attic room with what you really, truly want. What will make you happy with yourself or others. What will give you pleasure. What will bring you joy.

Don't laugh! You'd be amazed at the power in this simple Interior Clean Up. You can make lists later of just how you're going to accomplish the dreams you allow into your clean and light-filled attic room. You may have to practice this process again and again. And do a lot of letting go in the mundane, everyday world as well.

One of the basic laws of the universe is that nature abhors a vacuum. So of course you have to clear out the old before you can let in the new.

A much younger friend of mine who kept on meditating and kept on meditating but couldn't seem to accomplish her dreams told me that whenever she cleaned out the attic room it would just fill up again.

"What do you hear when you do the exercise?" I asked her.

"I keep being told to clean up my mess," she said. "So I do the exercise again and again, but nothing happens."

She lived in clutter and in chaos.

"Maybe you should really clean up the mess," I suggested. "Throw out the old magazines, clean out the closets, have a garage sale."

"But that would take time away from my spiritual life," she protested.

Yeah, right! How could joy rush into such disorder? Whenever I'm stuck or resisting or nothing good seems to be happening, I clean out my closets. After I get through deadlines and current projects, of course. And always before I start on a major work, as well. It always works.

Thought equals emotion equals action. When you allow more space in your life, there's more room to move around, to negotiate, to allow. And always, when you let go of all you do not want or need, there's room for all your new and glorious and unexpected good to rush in.

Don't take my word for it.

Just do it.

And throw out the refrigerator of your childhood as well.

The Worry Wolf

My mother is the champion worrier in our family. Practice makes perfect, and she has perfected the art. I learned to worry at my mother's knee. Sound familiar?

There's no use trying to change something so ingrained in her character. Sometimes I think she's even proud of it. "Well, that's just the way I *am*!" she declares proudly.

Well, that's just the way I'm *not*. Not anymore.

Sometimes I run with the wolves, hair streaming out behind me in the wind, creative juices flowing (metaphorically speaking). But sometimes, and more often than not as I get older, I come face to face with the worry wolf. He is large and grizzled gray and silver, with a ferocious snout and a manic gleam in his yellow eyes, and he scratches at my door with nails outstretched from his paws, and he howls to me, "Let me in."

I won't.

Because if I ever did, then I might as well give up on my creative dream. There's absolutely no use being a writer or any other self-employed person if you let the worry wolf eat you for lunch. I call it the worry wolf because it helps me to identify and separate myself from the anxiety and frustration and, yes, just plain fear that accompanies anyone who dances to a different drummer, reports on it, and expects to be rewarded by society for her observations.

Of course you can't ignore the worry wolf. When you've been paid only a few times a year, and once, for an awful, heart-stopping period, nothing for two years at all, then sometimes it's hard to shut your ears to the worry wolf howling at your door.

But you must.

I've found some ways to do this. First, you have to face your fear. No, don't open the door to the worry wolf! It's too hard to close it once he has sidled in. But when the howling gets to you, face the fear. Say it aloud, write it down, take a walk with it, cry if you must, grit your teeth if you will. Know while you're doing this that this is only the first step, not the final one. You can even shout at the worry wolf (this works best in the shower) and let your fear run down the drain.

First you notice that the worry wolf is indeed at your door again, pounding and scratching to get in. After acknowledging his presence, you can start to identify what's behind the worry. Is it fear? Or just discontent, irritation, frustration? How about rage?

Some friends I know always want to skip this part of the process. They tell me that they are worried, but afraid to take the next step, to go on into the emotion and then let it go. So they stuff the worry instead. That never works. The worry wolf will not be contained.

A very practical friend of mine tells me to make lists. I do. She calls it "running the numbers." It helps. You can do concrete planning when you make lists. You can put your emotions into action then. But if I make my lists or consider my options or make a plan too fast, without considering my emotions first, I just get depressed. And then the worry wolf howls louder at my door.

Another friend tells me to deal with what is. This advice sounds practical as can be, but first you have to figure out what's going on and why the worry wolf has shown his snout again, and then you can look at your options and your energy level as well. Because it does no good to just worry. It's draining and nonproductive. And of course you need your energy for other things.

It's part of my plan, when the worry wolf howls, to take the time to work through the emotions that the worry wolf engenders. Because he cannot be ignored. And he can't be petted, called soothing names, and let into your house. You have to do your dance even as he snarls and scratches on the other side of the door.

And when you do, acknowledging and expressing and feeling and letting out, and then listing the options and making a plan, then and only then does the energy change. And the emotions shift, and the project sells, and the check is in the mail. And only then and not a moment before does the worry wolf cease his howling and his scratching. He slinks away, disconsolate.

And you're home safe and free.

The Undefended Self

One of the characters in a novel I wrote tells her cousin as she lies dying, "I no longer have to defend against."

I remember that when I wrote that line I had spent years fighting the world. No matter how hard I tried, no matter how hard I worked, no matter how I loved or prayed—no matter what!—it seemed to me that I was still always defending myself. I was defending my back. I was covering my rear. I was armored. Mostly I was defending myself against the hurtful, wearying situations in which I found myself. Or so I thought.

I'm not the only writer to talk about the defended self. It's a traditional figure in literature, even in children's stories—remember the Tin Man in *The Wizard of Oz*, looking for a heart, but stuck within a rusted tin can of a body? That's a gentle example.

In classic psychoanalytic literature and most of the popular self-help books on the market, the defended self is a staple. Depending on what therapy is in vogue at the time, more or less emphasis is given to the pros and cons, the rights or wrongs, the "appropriateness" of the defended self. But no one tells us exactly how to go about transforming the defended self into the undefended self. Or tells us why we should even want this transformation.

It's easy to say: "Surrender. Surrender to the will of God. Surrender to rest, to sleep, to the way the world works. Rest and be thankful. Let go and let God." You know the drill.

I couldn't. I didn't know how. I was a ram battering my head against the immovable objects and people in my path. Survival at the price of continual vigilance. Sound familiar? You bet.

I was always taught that if you loved enough, you would be loved back. I tried unconditional love for years and years, and while it was undeniably good for my character, it played havoc with my emotions. After all, no matter how much I loved, people left. People sickened. People died. Was I fighting death or God? They got mixed up in my mind. Every time I tried to sort it all out, grief and rage came and got me by the throat and wouldn't let go. So I had a grudge against God. Try defending *that* position!

A night came when I could no longer go on. Not one more step. Not one more tear.

And no one came down on a cloud to rescue me. No, it wasn't like that at all.

Instead of asking for people, places, and things to change, instead of asking for angels and archangels and God and all the company of heaven to change, I asked that *I* be changed. And that was all. No trumpets sounding, no light swooping me up to heaven, no angels descending and ascending. No miracle.

Except. Except that my heart eased a little. And peace came trembling into a crevice I had left unguarded. And I discovered, somehow, in the days that followed, that there was a part of me so vulnerable, so loving, so gentle, so undefended, underneath the pain.

And I began to allow that part of me to blossom forth, a tiny bit at a time, like a rose in the heart that has been all thorns and a tight, closed bud, that now begins to open forth into its full-grown, natural splendor.

I'm shy about telling this. It's not something I usually share with the world. But I am less defended now, less armored, less closed in. I tell the truth more deeply and more clearly. I fear less. I love more. I am changed at depth.

And I'm still blossoming.

Waiting for the Rope to Come

I don't necessarily think of a rope as something to hang myself with or even something to be at the end of. Instead, when I think of popular clichés, folk wisdom that has stood the test of time, I think of a rope as something to reach for when all else fails and you're hanging on the cliff with bare hands and scraped knuckles and torn fingernails. That's when you need a rope to haul you back up the cliff.

We all have times when we come to the edge of a cliff and we fall a little way down and shout for help. It's a classic scene in American moviemaking, isn't it? Think of all the Saturday morning serials where the heroine is holding on to the edge of the cliff with her bare hands, shouting "Help!"

The Perils of Pauline. We were raised on images like that.

Well, you and I know she is going to be rescued in the last reel by the handsome cowboy/sheriff/passing hero, and so we can enjoy the suspense, knowing that she will not fall, knowing that she will be rescued in the nick of time. Whew! That was a close one!

Hasn't the same thing happened to you? You're fretting about timing, your manifestation has gone awry, delay is your middle name. All of a sudden, for no discernible reason you can point to, you find yourself hanging by your fingernails off the edge of the cliff, waiting for the rope to come.

And sometimes, no matter how hard you yell, no matter how brave and resilient you are, this is what happens: someone comes to the edge of the cliff, peers over, and tells you that the rope will come.

"Oh thank you!" you manage to gulp, dashing the melodramatic and maidenly tears away with one flick of your head. Oops, don't fall now! And then you ask the only question left: "When?"

"Oh, shouldn't be more than a week or two. Three, tops. So just hang on, little lady, for the rope is surely going to come."

"Three weeks!" You'd gnaw at your knuckles, you really would, but they are already white with fright and busy hanging on to the last little tree growing out of the crevice on the cliff face.

So you think to yourself, well, I might as well enjoy the view while I'm waiting. And you crane your neck a little and watch the sunset and the valley below and try to estimate how far down it is to fall. You watch the birds and the clouds and the wildflowers growing in the crevices of the cliff, and you hum a little tune to yourself to keep your spirits up, something that will harmonize with the words of *The Little Engine That Could*: "I think I can, I think I can, oh my yes, I think I can." And you hold on a little longer. Waiting.

The sunset fades and the stars come out, and it gets colder on the cliff. You whistle in the dark.

Wondering when the rope will come.

Timing is everything.

Other People's Dreams

I've almost perfected my dreaming abilities. I have years of journals with recorded dreams. I know the techniques. I've taught classes in dreaming and written about dreams. My own private royal road to the unconscious has served me well. From its rich bed I draw inspiration and ideas for my creative work. I uncover and discover who I am and where I've been and what I need to know and where I'm going.

I've dreamed other people's dreams as well. Both waking and sleeping. I have lived other people's dreams.

I even started my publishing company to fulfill my son's dream, not mine. I carried that dream mission of his around inside of me for years. I held its energy and its vision. Until it faltered when the energy died. It was a valuable time for me. I learned a lot. I won't do it just that way again.

When the man I had been married to for eighteen years and divorced from for three died, I began to dream his dreams. I followed his path into hell and back night after night. He died forgiven, but unforgiving. We had to work out all that was unresolved between us through his dreams. It took professional help and time to do this. Because he haunted me.

And I still dream other people's dreams. When my mother was ill, I dreamed the same dreams she did. Her mother, my beloved grandmother, would come to her when she was awake. She would see her form and hear her voice. But for me, my grandmother came to me in dreams. She comforted us both.

Visionaries and mystics and channelers dream planetary dreams. Psychics dream the dreams of celebrities or murderers and see how some other person's life will unfold. Some of it is common sense and guessing, of course. Some of it is strange and odd and wild, tapping into the future with intense emotion.

Writers dream characters and plots into being. Artists dream pictures. Inventors dream their way into new products. There is, of course, the cultural dream, the hypnotized societal dream we fall into when we are unconscious or have been watching too much television.

Time folds back upon itself in dreams. We learn where we have been and what we really think. We work out our pasts, our present, and our future in our dreams.

Sometimes we discover, as I did, that we have been dreaming other people's dreams. Sometimes we discover that we have been making other people's dreams come true, instead of our own. Sometimes we discover that we have been living someone else's dream. Sometimes we even discover that we are in the wrong dream. Then we have to cut ourselves loose into waking life. Into what is "real."

And yet, I have always known that dreams, my own and others, are just as real as everyday three-dimensional facts and figures, and just as solid as bodies, jobs, houses, and cars. I could not be a writer if I did not know that first there is the dream and then there is the concrete, finite manifestation of the dream.

In dreams begin realities.

Whose reality are you dreaming?

Can you now dream your own?

Opening
the
Heart

LISTEN,

LISTEN, LISTEN,

TO MY HEART'S

SONG

Opening the Heart

Much has been written about preparing the heart, opening the heart, living from the heart. But hardly anybody ever tells you how.

I remember jogging in the park years ago. As I ran, the echo of a memory came to me like a song. And so I chanted under my breath as I ran. "Listen, listen, listen, to my heart's song." That was all. Over and over again that whole year I chanted "Listen, listen, listen, to my heart's song" in rhythm with the running of my feet. And my heart, whether from the running or the echo of the phrase, began to open in unison with my breath.

Later, more words came to me. I don't know if you would call this a poem, a prayer, or a song. I don't know your heart. Nor would I presume to tell anyone how to pray, or by what name to call the divine source they yearn toward with every fiber of their being, with every step they take. Here is the prayer that helped me to open my heart. A simple song to my Creator. So that later, when challenges came, my heart was open enough to be of help to those I loved. This I chanted daily:

> *Open my heart, that I may see,*
> > *visions of good You have for me.*

> *Open my heart, that I may hear*
> > *Your love and wisdom guiding me clearly.*

> *Open my heart, that I may feel,*
> > *all that is true, all that is real.*

> *Open my heart, that I may know,*
> > *what I must do and where I must go.*

> *Open my heart, that I may be*
> > *Whatever, in love, You want me to be.*

Then I would breathe in and out through my breastbone, the fourth spiritual center, the heart center. I would inhale love and then I would exhale love as I went about my day.

This is not a pious primer. I cannot do anything other than to suggest, gently, that mind is not all there is. That body is not all there is. That spirit, so often seeming far away and beyond our grasp and understanding, requires no saints to do its work in the world. Perhaps all that is required is an opening, opening, ever-opening heart in order to do the work of the soul in the rhythm of the everyday world. Listen! You may hear your own heart's song.

Tending the Wounded

Nothing has ever opened my heart so quickly, so completely, as living through seven years of the AIDS crisis. My heart broke open and stayed open. From early 1985 until the end of 1992, when I finished my fourth book, a novel about AIDS, after three related books on loss, dying, and grief recovery, I served, like hundreds and thousands of others, in this struggle against a plague that seems as yet to have no ending. And I wrote about it. These words are from my novel *Families*.

Into this plague I came, both innocent and ignorant. Into this cauldron of fear, rage, loss, grief, guilt, I came.

I was, at the time, a middle-aged, middle-class writer from Texas, not a rebel, never an activist. I was neither nurse nor doctor, neither social worker nor psychiatrist. I was simply an ordinary woman whose son was dying.

I came to take care. I stayed to care. I stayed

for seven years. And I will never be the same again.

I was not an observer. I was a participant. And everything that happened to me and the ones I loved is etched indelibly on my mind and in my body.

This plague changed the world. Those of us who served are all changed utterly. We can never go back to being the people we once were. The past is dead. Who we were has disappeared. Innocence has fled forever. Indifference finds no home here.

Those of us who are still alive are survivors in a plague with no ending. We endure. We serve. We attempt to stem the tide of an ocean of pain that keeps on coming. Our sons and daughters, husbands, wives, friends, lovers are scattered bones and ashes in that deep, that ocean with no ending.

We are not swept out to sea. We receive no such mercy. We are the caregivers. We stay on the shore and tend the wounded.

What is the lesson here? Surely there is a life lesson, or two or three or more, to be learned out of every tragedy. Otherwise, nothing makes sense.

Here are some lessons I learned. But at what cost!

I learned that families can come together in love, no matter their disparate lifestyles, no matter their unresolved agendas, when a luminous soul draws them together in a circle of unconditional love. I learned that other people's opinions, whether born out of ignorance, indifference, cruelty, or bigotry, have no relevance. I learned that actions of love eclipse rhetoric. I learned that the personal is the political, and the personal is the universal, and that even when hearts break, they can serve. Indeed they must. I learned the power of emotions to fuel the words forward, so that the meaning behind the words can touch others and help them to understand and to care. I learned that human beings are both stronger and wiser than I ever dreamed they were. I learned that love lasts beyond bodies. I learned about the essence shining out from within and beyond the body. I learned about the soul.

So yes, I am changed forever by my son's journey. It has been an integral part of my own journey.

I no longer stay on the shore and tend the wounded. Caregivers get tired and burnt-out, or "AIDSed-out" as they call it in the jargon of the movement. But I still serve.

Opening the heart is not a pious-sounding platitude. It is a perilous journey indeed. It requires a deepening and a strengthening, as well as a widening. The rewards are nothing less than the practice of unconditional love. But you will be changed at depth. You will be changed forever.

I came home from a war and I survived. But it changed my life. And just as I am a part of all that I have met, I am a part of all that I have written, and I am a part of all that I have mourned. I am a part of all that I have loved. And that's what opening the heart is. To be a part of all that you have ever loved. And to continue loving. At whatever cost.

Silver Threads

Recently the echo of an old, debilitating illness came round my door again. It didn't stay long. I am sturdier now and far less stressed than when it first reared its ugly head ten years ago. But as a consequence of its reappearance in my life, I was required to do a six-week clearing program, to root out old infections, old toxins, old allergies. And as a further consequence, I was told not to tint my hair. Not tint my hair! It's already three weeks overdue. When can I color it again to just that shade of sunshine with red highlights it used to have when I was young?

"Never," said my doctor. "I strongly suggest no more chemicals poured into an already altogether too sensitive body."

Well! I thought I had made peace with my body, although I still yearned for more lightness in each step. I even laughed about the typeface on my computer, enlarged so that I could see each sentence more easily as I wrote. I thought I had made peace with the encroaching years. Oh vanity! My crowning glory gone.

To cheer myself up, I drove out into the country on a Saturday afternoon to see my best friend of almost thirty years. A no-nonsense Texas woman who, in her long and varied life, has been a school psychologist and a legal mediator and now runs a construction company her late husband built.

So there we were, standing out on the prairie on a sunny spring afternoon, her large country house on the hill behind us, a view of the city spread out miles away. To a casual observer, it might have looked like a picture from the thirties or the forties, torn from a scrapbook. If we squinted against the sun, we might have thought we were our mothers, two women of indeterminate age gossiping in a yard.

The wind played havoc with my hair. "Oh," my friend exclaimed, "I love the way the silver in your hair shines in the sunlight."

I began laughing. "And I love the way your face wrinkles when you smile," I said to her. "It makes your face so-o-o interesting."

We almost fell to the ground laughing. "I love your shoes, my dear," she cried.

"The latest fashion," I replied. I was wearing my clumpy, galumpy walking shoes with the custom orthotics, because of an old foot injury. "Old lady shoes" we used to call them, my friends and I, as we once teetered into offices on high heels.

"Investment dressing not required," I said to her, pointing at her divided skirt and ample top.

"Makeup not required," she yelled back at me in the wind, as I could almost feel the freckles popping out upon my skin.

We began prancing around the yard, yelling at one another, laughing all the while. If the radio had burst just then into a country western song, I wouldn't have been surprised at all if we had do-si-doed our way around her acre. We capered, we giggled, we shouted endearments and insults.

"Silver threads among the gold," she cried to me as her final shot, as I got into my car.

"The best years are the last years," I called back.

Old age is fun with friends.

Alphabet Soup

I'm visiting my oldest son and his family. Two of my granddaughters are sitting at their play table with me. We are sipping soup. Alphabet soup.

Callie, who is six, is learning to read. We have already read *The Cat in the Hat* at least three times today, and it's only lunchtime. I point out the letters in the soup to her. In her advanced Californian first grade, she is learning both English and Spanish. Zoe, her younger sister, is four. She is fascinated with the shapes and the textures and the colors. She stirs her spoon dreamily. Zoe is almost always in her own world, with its private symbols.

"Look girls!" I say to them. "Can you find your names in the soup? Can you spell out the words?"

Callie, who loves logic and routine, who is methodical in all she does, stares intently at the soup, figuring out its terrain. These letters are not in a book. Therefore, she is suspicious that they exist. Zoe, quicksilver and intense, stirs and stirs, daring the soup to yield up its mysteries.

I explain to them that there are twenty-six letters in the English alphabet. We try to find each one, lifting the letters carefully onto a waiting plate. Callie sounds them out one by one. Zoe eats the Z.

I'm really getting into the game. Like a child, I arrange the slippery letters. The English language is made up of twenty-six symbols that make words, speech, language, stories, books. Communication. The information superhighway in alphabet soup. Twenty-six symbols in infinite arrangements that the eye and the brain translate into feelings and thoughts and whole worlds of imagination.

My own writing has not been going well. What do I have to say, after all, that hasn't been said by others, in various languages, many times, and probably better? And yet twenty-six letters to arrange and rearrange into words that connect with others, words that inspire, move, illuminate, teach, entertain, touch, and change the minds and hearts of others.

Suddenly, with a rift of memory, I am back in Mexico City, in a time when my own sons were both younger and older than the two girls sitting here. I am teaching in a private school, where students from all over the world learn Spanish in the morning and English in the afternoon. All the subjects are taught in two languages, repeated and reiterated in order for the students to think in both languages. I am beginning to dream in Spanish, even though I have been in Mexico City for only a few weeks.

I remember being called from my classroom down to the kindergarten, where my second oldest son, John, a first-grader, is on strike. There he sits, arms folded stubbornly across his chest, pencil broken, paper wadded up in front of him on the desk. His elderly, authoritarian teacher is wringing her hands. A torrent of Spanish pours from her lips. He has been disobedient, he won't cooperate, look at all the other children sitting so nicely in their school uniforms, making marks on the page. I must take him home. I must punish him.

John sets his mouth in a stubborn line and lets the words wash over him. I kneel at his desk. "What's wrong?" I ask him.

His head comes up a trifle. There are tears in his eyes. "Mama," he says in despair, "get me out of here. The words won't work."

So we end up learning Spanish together, John and I. All those words! All those books and tutors! Degrees have been conferred along the way for both of us in languages learned and half-forgotten.

Once I wrote bilingual textbooks and bilingual children's books. Now I am lucky if I can get the words to work in my own native tongue. Now I am lucky if I can help my granddaughters to find their names in alphabet soup.

I still dream in Spanish, when I am tired. And how amazing it is, to me at least, that I make my living by arranging and rearranging the letters in alphabet soup. So you can read them now.

Sometimes the words work after all.

Forgiving and Forgetting

We women have been told by most of the psychologists on the planet that whenever something terrible happens in our lives, the trick is to forgive and to forget. No matter the origin of the trauma, no matter the severity or length of the tragedy or difficulty or shock, we must, must, must, without fail and as soon as possible, both forgive and forget.

Otherwise we're stuck, rigid, unbending, nonfunctioning, and not too nice to be around.

I was sitting around the kitchen table with some friends one day, and they all agreed that forgiving is easy, but forgetting is hard.

One woman quoted Eleanor Roosevelt, her hero and her icon, who had said essentially the same thing, as she accompanied her husband's body across the country to lie at last in state. "I can forgive, but how do I forget?"

Each woman had a horror story or two or three to tell. They wanted to go on, they knew they had to go on, they were all magnificent, fully functioning, courageous women who had in fact gone on, and yet they wrestled with their memories. They were afraid that they would never be able to do it right, that is, to forget the past, as well as forgiving it.

But I don't think that you should forget the past. I don't think you can. You are your past. You are your memories. You can forgive, that's not so hard. It's essential, so that baggage doesn't collect like a ball and chain around your ankles and make you a prisoner of your past. But I don't think you can forget all that has made you who you are. All that has taught you. Like childbirth, you forget the pain, yes, but you keep the result of the pain. You birth a new being into the world.

One of my friends, a wise counselor with a wealth of experiences that might have crushed a more fragile woman, told me that she refuses to forget her husband's long battle with cancer.

"It was an important part of our life together. I won't forget his death, just like I won't forget all the good years we had together. I won't forget any of it."

You can't make me forget. You cannot take my memories. I am my memories. Oh, I can forget the pain, but never the intensity, the intimacy, the immediacy. Oh, I can forgive God, the disease, other people, myself, fate, circumstance.

Name something, anything, and I can forgive. But I will not forget. Because my memories are me. They have shaped me in this world. From the time I first learned to walk and talk and move about in the world, I have used my senses to remember how to do each task, how to learn each lesson, how to feel and how to love, and how to work and how to serve. How to give birth and how to let go with grace when the dying is done. I am a part of all that I have met and all that I have felt. So do not ask me to forget. Even if it is uncomfortable for those around me. Even if it hurts. Don't ask me to forget. Not one moment! Each moment made me who I am now. Each moment made me wise.

So we women, seated around a kitchen table, can tell horror stories and sorrow stories. We can laugh at our foolishness concerning ex-husbands or erring teenagers, we can ask for ways and means to release resentments about work or money or ex-bosses. We can remember the dear ones we have lost. We can ask how to forgive, and when to forgive. We can ask for absolution. We can ask for comfort, caring, love, understanding, relief.

But do not ask us to forget.

Hanging the Teabags Out to Dry

My maternal grandmother, my mother, her two sisters, an elderly female relative, a female friend and boarder, and four little girls of varying ages all lived together during the Depression and the Second World War. Ten women living in a commodious, three-story Victorian house in a southern town. The men in our lives had either died earlier or gone to war. So I was shaped by three generations of well-bred, educated, hardworking women making do. There was no lack of love, manners, attention, education, or instruction in that life. But we were frugal folk. We neither wasted nor wanted. We were careful, thrifty, reasonably content. We knew value.

When I talk with other women of my generation and the one before, I find much the same story. Extravagance was not an option. But we knew who we were, from what pioneer stock we had sprung, and so we felt little lack within ourselves, no matter the economies necessary to survive.

Once, before my beloved grandmother died, my mother and I took her to a play. There were two characters in the play, a mother and a daughter, southern country women, in the middle of the Depression, who, in order to have enough when company came to call, took their used teabags and hung them on a clothesline and redunked them when company came for tea.

I thought my grandmother would split her sides laughing. We practically had to carry her home. I didn't see what was so funny. I was still very young. I vowed to be rich and famous, to escape whatever rules, regulations, mannerisms, and customs had been instilled in me by my foremothers. I would never make a joke of poverty. I would have everything and do everything and be everything.

I would never hang the teabags out to dry.

This vow carried me through an incredibly varied array of ups and downs on the financial ladder of life. There were years in which I struggled to clothe and house my children. There were years in which I lived a life of modest comfort. There were years in which I discovered that I had a head for business as well as poetry. There were years when the money rolled in, and I learned how the economic world worked.

There is no lack in my life. Family and friends surround me. Books and food, ideas and creativity are in abundance. I have time and energy. My responsibilities and surroundings are by conscious choice, after much floundering in the sea of infinite choices.

And yes, like my grandmother, I am thrifty and frugal. Old habits die hard. Oh, I use china cups and fresh unused teabags when people come to call. I put out cookies on flowered plates, like all good southern women of my generation. I ply my friends with food and attention. I begrudge nothing.

Yet when everyone has gone home, what do I do? Guess.

Do you know that you can get at least four cups of tea from one teabag? Sometimes five, if the water is hot enough. I do this every morning and every night. And then I lift the soggy teabag onto a separate dish so that it can dry and be used again.

Ritual evokes memory.

I still hear my grandmother laughing.

The Well-Used Hearts of Men

It is easy for me to talk about the heart of a woman. How well I know the easy lovingness of friends, colleagues, mentors, kin.

But I am baffled by men's hearts. I am shy as well, not having loved altogether wisely through two very long marriages and one or two other encounters in my time. For a modern woman, I am unsophisticated. So who am I to talk about men's hearts?

I have four sons.

When I let memory lead me to what I know about men's hearts, I see vignettes, small stories and pictures that capture, for my heart, what I know of the four men I love best.

When I think of my oldest son, Bill, I remember a time a few Christmases ago, when after much frustration, pounding, noise, and swearing on Christmas Eve my son acknowledged that the jungle gym he had bought for Santa Claus to give to his two preschool daughters was beyond his capacity to assemble. He just sat down and cried. (Oh tender-hearted Bill!)

Meanwhile, my mother, daughter-in-law, and I quickly unwrapped the presents we had wrapped earlier and spread them out along the fireplace, so that the little girls would see these alternate gifts from Santa when they awoke in the morning.

And this is what my son did. He wrote a letter to his daughters from Santa Claus. In it, he explained that Santa couldn't get the jungle gym down the chimney without singeing his suit, and that Santa had so many toys to deliver to good little boys and girls that he had asked the girls' daddy to put the surprise together the next day, and that they had indeed been good little girls the whole year.

"But do you think," he asked us earnestly, "that they will know how much I love them?"

"Yes, Bill, they will," we all chorused in reply.

The next day the girls watched, clapping their hands and shouting "oooh," as my oldest son, my teenage grandson, and my youngest son spent hours assembling Santa's surprise.

My oldest son has a well-used heart.

When I think of that youngest son of mine, Robert, I remember the time he took off work and came to my office and held my hand while I cried and explained to my staff that the publishing company I had started six years earlier was closing for good. And I remember, as well, the time he and I decided to move my mother, his grandmother, into a new place to live. "I'll help you, Mother," he said. "I want Grandmother to have a safe, warm, cozy place."

My youngest son has a well-used heart.

My second son, John, is a quiet, mellow outdoorsman. What I remember, when I close my eyes and think of him, is a scene etched indelibly in my memory. I am holding my son, Michael, half-upright in bed, while John lovingly washes his dying brother's body, with tenderness in every stroke of the washcloth, making small jokes all the while, so as not to embarrass Michael.

My son John has a well-used heart.

One scene I will never forget took place about three weeks before Michael died. He sat in a wheelchair by the fireplace, with an Indian shawl over his shoulders, and he and I and the part of the family that was there with him drank golden wine as Michael toasted "to life!" And we pretended that it was another Christmas yet to come and opened presents in July.

My son Michael had a well-used heart.

These are not mere sentimental musings. They are a love letter from me to men I have known that have helped me to recognize love, in all its shapes and forms, guises and disguises. I could give you a hundred more examples, if you had the time.

When my sons were teenagers, they thought that I was a terrible mother. They have since changed their minds. When I was younger, I thought that I could never fathom the mystery of a man's heart. But I am older and wiser now. And so are they. Tenderness has long since replaced rebellion.

I always wanted people to recognize and respond to my work. My writing life was something I snatched at sporadically over a period of years in between raising four sons. Now I would be honored if someone said to me, "You have raised loving sons." That was my work too.

And I have four sons with well-used hearts.

Tennis Shoes in the Rain

I was driving along in downtown Santa Monica with a friend after a meditation class. She was actually more than a friend. This dynamic and beautiful woman was my minister as well, and we had experienced the class together. I always seem to find wonderful women ministers in my life.

We were driving along in the rain, on the way to my apartment, volleying abstract concepts and ideas about our spiritual paths back and forth in the car. It had been a casual weeknight class, and my friend had on a pink sweat suit with matching pink tennis shoes. The rage that year was all for decoration. The tennis shoes were a marvel, hand-painted, with stars appliquéd upon them.

We stopped at a street crossing, and all of a sudden we both fell silent. A woman was passing who could have been our age or older, there was no way to tell. She shuffled across at the light, her gray hair plastered to her skull, her clothes mismatched. She was pushing a shopping cart filled with all her belongings. She was barefoot.

My friend stopped the car. "Be right back," she said. She leapt out into the rain, ran through the puddles, then took off her own hand-painted, star-appliquéd pink tennis shoes and held them out to the homeless woman.

The woman hesitated, then grabbed them and held them to her chest. Then she reached out to my friend. I thought she might attack her or embrace her. But no, she was merely steadying herself with a hand on my friend's shoulder, as she slowly put on first one shoe and then another. She stamped her feet into the puddles to see if the shoes fit. They did. She grimaced or smiled, I couldn't tell which. Then she walked off into the night with a wave of her hand.

My friend ran back to the car. Her own hair was plastered to her skull. She was wet and shivering. She pumped the gas pedal with one of her wet, bare feet. We drove on.

She began to cry. "There but for the grace of God go I," she said.

"Me too," I answered softly.

Then she stopped again, and we sat in the car and talked. She poured out all her longings and frustrations, her personal feelings that she had never shared with a member of her congregation. I listened. She had troubles I had never even dreamed of. We cried together in the rain. She went homeward, as did I. We never spoke of it again.

But when I think that I am the only person in the world to be visited by trouble, I think of that night when my friend, my stoic, spiritual woman friend, gave away her new pink tennis shoes and shared her pain with me.

We are all ministers to one another.

The Four Sacred Things

The shamanic tradition of the indigenous people of both North and South America contains a spiritual system for looking at the world as a sacred grid. This blueprint incorporates symbols of nature, the elements, power animals, and myth to construct a vision of the world. What follows is a simplified version of the four sacred things.

Here are the four sacred things:
Earth, Air, Fire, Water.

Here are the four sacred directions:
North, East, South, West.

Here are the four symbols of the four sacred directions:

• In the North, there is the dragon path. This path is the way to discover the wisdom of the ancients and to create a union with the divine.

- In the East, there is the eagle path. This path is the flight to the sun and the journey back to your home to exercise your vision within your chosen life and work.

- In the South, there is the serpent path, where you go to shed your past, as a serpent sheds its tail.

- In the West, there is the jaguar path. On the jaguar path, you lose all fear and face the change of worlds we call death.

Whatever your country, culture, race, religion, or gender, the symbolic directions inherent in the four sacred things can be a spiritual geography for the seeker.

What is your path? Where are you in direction, vision, dream, accomplishment? What have you mastered? What have you yet to learn? Where do you need to go next on your path? What is awaiting you?

There is a fifth sacred thing as well. Some call it the Ether. Some call it the Power. Some call it the Spirit.

But the fifth sacred thing is Love.

The Compassionate Self

There is a woman who comes to me in dreams. Both those when I am sleeping and those when I'm awake. In meditation she comes to me and sometimes in prayer. I feel her presence around me more often now of late. I have known her for a very long time.

Her name is Persea, which means "of the sea." She is surrounded by gold and blue light. She is taller than I am, with white skin and long dark hair. She looks nothing like me. She is dressed in white robes, toga-style, and her hair and waist are tied with braided colors. She is more than a wraith, a ghost, or an apparition. For she is strong and sturdy and noble and calm and wise. She brings to me all those qualities for which I long.

Years ago, I wanted to offer other women something of what I had then glimpsed only briefly and had never acknowledged up to that time. I wrote of a woman whom I called "the compassionate self." I had no compassion for myself back then. This was a time when I wanted to fix myself, I wanted to change my image, I wanted to change my body, I wanted to change my surroundings. I wanted to change my life! I did not dare to do so then, although surely Persea helped me to see that someone cared about me, even in the midst of my confused struggles.

"Be careful what you wish for," the old folktales say, "for you will surely get it." I wanted to change myself and change my life. I got it.

In my meditations this figure, this woman out of time, came to me, rising out of a pond, rising out of a lake, rising out of a river, finally at last, irrevocably, rising out of the sea. She came to me out of water, the deep, the unconscious, the depths. She rose up and walked on water. She beckoned me to do the same.

I was never afraid of her. In fact, in my meditations I called her "the compassionate self" because I yearned so for just such as she to give me compassion, to fill me up. I yearned then for someone, anyone, to care about me, just as I was then, gasping like a fish out of water, dry, arid, but with torrents within. I longed for someone to take the hooks out of my flesh and rescue me from the barren, sandy shore, to take me in her arms, soothe me with the water that poured from those arms, and gently carry me into the sea, that blue and gold rhythmic sea, where I could swim joyously, freely, where I would not drown. Where I would never drown, because Persea, she of the sea itself, would abide with me.

Was Persea a vision? A past life bleed-through? A ghost? A higher self? A lower self? A goddess? An angel? A friend? An archetype? A myth? There are so many fancies that we take, we women, as we gasp for air and struggle for our lives, our own unique, wise, creative, passionate lives.

She was, perhaps, all of the above, although I cannot prove it. She who once stood outside of me, rising alone from the water, her caring hands outstretched to me, is outside no more. She has taken root within me now, this aspect of my-self, this mythic woman. She is all and more than I have ever wished to be. She is within. Within me. Now. She is more than me. She is the helper, the friend, the muse. She is uncondi-tional love. She is wisdom made manifest. She is the compas-sionate self.

Find yours. By any name at all, call her. She will not deny you. She is waiting for your call. Allow her to come to you. Allow her to nurture and nourish and hold you in her care. Allow her in. Then you and she will rise together out of

the depths of the blue and gold sea. Allow her in. Be comforted. Be guided. Be made whole. Be soul.

Love and Sex in Fragrant Combination

Like many long-lived women who came of age in the fifties, my experiences of love and sex have changed as the decades have changed. And like many women I know, I have experienced both sex without love and love without sex. We women want them both together, the loving of men and the intimacy and the passion and the celebration and the friendship as well. Sometimes we get lucky. I did. Once.

It was after a long and bitter divorce, after I had made great changes in my life, but before I had worked through grief and rage at eighteen years gone awry.

Then he showed up. Like an angel falling out of the clear blue sky, he appeared. You've heard of counterparts, haven't you? Twin souls, twin flames? I wasn't looking for anyone at all (isn't that always the way?) but he showed up anyway and helped me to be whole.

Let me tell you about this extraordinary man. This kind, unassuming, middle-aged, short, wiry widower, balding with soft brown curly hair, this man who dressed to please himself, not others, this poet, editor, painter, traveler, this man of astonishing intellect, brooding melancholy, intense passion. A meditator, a reader, a profound thinker. This wild creative soul. Well, don't you think I thought I had met my double?

I remember that we fit together perfectly, top to toe and all points in between. Love and sex in fragrant combination. (The rest is private.)

For reasons too complicated and convoluted to explain in anything less than a full-length novel, I went to California, not knowing at the time that a six-month sojourn would lengthen into seven years. I went to California and he found someone else. End of story. The last time I heard from him was when he wrote me a beautiful letter after my son had died. I still have the letter, tucked away in my box of treasures.

We used to walk for hours across the fields and parks, our arms around each other, and if this were fantasy there would be an ending with the sound of violins and this man and I running across a meadow into each other's arms.

It didn't happen that way. The timing was all wrong. He disappeared from my life as thoroughly and completely as if the sky had taken him back.

"Words called regret gain no momentum here." That was the line of a poem I had written that I read to him. We used to read poetry to each other in bed—his, mine—and Yeats as well. Oh, it was perfect! While it lasted. I grow dizzy with remembering.

That was ten years ago. He'd be in his sixties now, an age when, as one of my friends says, "Good men are like fine wine, to be sipped and savored." I'd like to savor him.

I am a lucky woman. I have experienced both love and sex together, with no compromises, no fear, no adjustments. I can remember how good a man and a woman can be together.

Sometimes a meditation is merely memory recalled. A memory of the best that love can be, for however long we are gifted with its blessing. "Words called regret gain no momentum here."

If by some chance we should ever meet again, no matter our ages then, no matter the circumstances, no matter the events leading us back together, if by some chance we should happen upon one another, this is what I would do. I would open my arms and draw him into me. And I would cherish him, all of him. Love and sex in fragrant combination.

And when all is said and done, no matter what happens, I regret nothing.

Alive

My cousin's husband was in the hospital for surgery. He had cancer. Complications ensued, and the hospital stay extended itself, with scary and weary emotions for all of us involved.

"I'll be there for you," I told my cousin and her husband, lending books and moral support, an occasional place for my cousin to lay her head, a shoulder to cry on, a shared meal or two. Surely that was all that was required of me. Surely, after years of working in the AIDS crisis, with death and dying, with support groups, with families, surely after years of caregiving I could be excused. I had done my share. I had put in my time. I had books to write, and places to go, and people to see, and joy to discover. So I told myself, as I shrank from the occasional obligatory hospital visit.

Then one afternoon, as I visited the hospital reluctantly but dutifully, I came upon my cousin's husband alone, staring out the window at the noisy, busy construction site below. Somehow, past the daily recital of symptoms and prognoses, he began talking about how people reconstruct their lives after a long crisis. About how people go on after pain and loss. About how ordinary people, like the people in my family, shine softly, leading the way, so that others may not stumble or fall quite so far into despair. I remember that we talked of courage and of everyday kindness.

A connection flowed between us. The hospital room lightened. Despair eased.

Then he asked me to do him a special favor. Would I give him a neck and back massage? He hurt so much.

I did as he asked. The side where the surgery had been, where the scars were, resisted my touch. It was cold, dark, clammy, despairing, shocked, numb. The side where no surgery had occurred, however, was warm to my touch. Alive. As I kneaded and pummeled and stroked, gently, so as not to hurt him, an amazing thing happened. The hurt, cut, ravaged side of his body warmed, ever so slightly. The healthy side of his body responded. A connection flowed between us again. I could almost see the energy.

Alive. A holy instant.

He thanked me courteously when I finished and fell back onto the pillow to sleep. " No indeed, thank *you*!" I responded.

I walked out of the hospital room and down the corridor, blinded by tears. I got into the car and cried old numb, scared, hurt places within me back to life.

Gifts given, gifts received.

Alive. I'm alive.

Dream-Catcher Woman

I wanted to catch a dream, find my vision, follow my path. I wanted signs and symbols, portents and promises. In short, I wanted to get out of my rut, my pounding at the computer day after day for over two years, with no outward and visible sign of success, of recognition, of respect. I wanted, in short, a miracle.

It didn't have to be a big one. No, rather a promise, a signpost, a marked path along a trail that indicated that yes, dreams do come true, yes, you are in your right time and space and work and place, yes, continue and all will be well.

The opportunity came within three days of wishing it. Isn't that always the way? I went to Taos, New Mexico, with a friend, a solid, warm, no-nonsense, substantial teacher friend from twenty years ago. We renewed our friendship, remembered the past, shared wisdoms, laughed like schoolgirls.

I continued to search for signs along the way. We came to the Enchanted Circle—a trio of mountain and lake and ski resorts that make a ring around the mountains. Red River, Angel Fire, Eagle's Nest. Even their names have power. At the top of the highest mountain, winding through the narrow mountain roads, I saw a trail off to the side. I wanted to follow it. We didn't stop, We didn't take the time. It said— I swear this is what it said— "Integration Point. Where eagles fly."

We came down onto the plateau. We had traveled from sea level to over 9000 feet high, and now back down to 7000 feet. The air was crisp, clean, dry as a bone. The air was tangy and sparkling. You could get drunk on the air alone. Vast empty distances, narrow roads, an intoxicating brew of desert and lakes, of mountain peaks and valley floors. The sky a brilliant, endless blue. Ah, it was magical! Into the town we drove, an ancient, tree-lined plaza, adobe walls, riotous flowers, art and silver everywhere. I felt I had come home.

There was more. We wished, my friend and I, for people to meet, for connections. I wished for a future where I could return here. I felt both grounded and accelerated to a feverish energy. I was dizzy, because of the altitude. We laughed a lot. We searched and ambled along the unexpected passageways that drew the eye to another and yet another shop, bookstore, art gallery, treasure trove, mysterious and yet bone-deep familiar vista.

We went to the Indian Pueblo. I found a golden web, an

intricate, lacy circle, with golden feathers hanging from its center.

"It's a dream-catcher," the woman who offered it to me said. I knew about dream-catchers. They were made of feathers and twigs and colors. They looked like woven tennis rackets, asymmetrical, with totems laid within their depths. You kept one over your bed.

"It's to keep the bad dreams away," the woman explained to my friend and me. "To keep the bad dreams away but let the good dreams through. Catch the good dreams. Let the others go."

But this dream-catcher was different from all the others. It called to me. It wasn't really gold, but gold-like, a kind of metal that would wear well along the way. I put it around my neck. It felt warm, solid, centered, grounded. It fit me.

We left the pueblo. Where to next? "Follow that road," I cried. All of this was astonishing, a way out of accustomed seeing and being. We left our practical, orderly, sedate, aging selves behind. We followed the road. I saw an eagle circling above us, leading our way.

"An Integration Point. Where eagles fly," I said to myself. "Stop here," I cried. "Take that road."

We went a dusty ten miles or so along a hidden, bone-jolting road. It led to unexpected treasure, a home of a famous writer, a lecture tour in progress, a guide, new friends. It led to private homes and foundations, grants-in-aid, work-in-progress, future work promised and planned.

When the day was done, I had a future. I had a golden thread that led me in a circle, an enchanted circle, that would, I hoped, in a not too far distant time, lead me again to this place I already called home.

I brought the golden-webbed dream-catcher home. I do not wear it every day. I only wear it when something wonderful, mysterious, unexpected, unexplained is about to happen. I feel it in my bones. Then I take the dream-catcher from off my desk, where it resides among my manuscripts, and I put it on and sally forth, knowing that in some out-of-ordinary time, out-of-ordinary space, I am a dream-catcher woman. And so I go forth to catch my dreams. I let the bad ones go. I keep only the good ones.

I'm returning to Taos next year, wearing my dream-catcher. I'll be looking for the eagle.

Waiting for the Gentle Man

I can't get this story out of my mind. I read it months ago in a writers' magazine. It haunts me. It's a true story.

It seems there was this well-known, respected writer (her name is not important) who for many years wrote books and articles and columns on prayer. She was published all over the world in religious and secular publications. She was famous.

It seems that after many years her husband died. No one knew that it was a desperately unhappy marriage. She had endured it for years. I think she was in her sixties when she became a widow. She stayed in the same house she had always lived in, where she had written her books of prayers, although she wrote no longer.

One day an elderly gentleman in another town, in another state, in another part of the country, lost his wife to some dread disease. To comfort him, he read the writer's prayers again and again, through the dying and then the grieving, he read the writer's prayers. They got him through.

One day he got on a plane, and, clutching the writer's books in one hand and a bouquet of flowers in the other, he showed up on the writer's doorstep. Yes! And he asked the writer to autograph the books that had given him so much solace and so much hope and so much pleasure.

"I feel I have always known you," he told her shyly.

She invited him into her parlor. Yes! She signed the books and put the flowers in a vase and offered him tea. They talked. He told her his life's story. She told him hers. Well, maybe not the first day, but you know what I mean.

Shortly thereafter, they married. This gentle man and gentle woman. I think that she declared he was her soul mate. I think that he declared he had been looking for her all his life. And they lived happily, blissfully, prayerfully, ever after.

The moral of this story is: Prayer works!

One more thing. Yes. Let me tell you, let me put it into a prayer and send it forth. It's just this. I'm waiting for that knock on the door. I will open it, and there on a sunny afternoon, will be a shy man, a gentleman, a good man, a reading man, a mellow, healthy, well-seasoned man. He will be holding my books in one hand and a bouquet of flowers in the other.

And I will invite him in.

Learning Through Joy

A wise friend of mine once told me that first we learn all of our lessons through pain. This is the way of the human being. We experiment. We experience. From our first baby steps to near the end of our current lives, we learn, generally, usually, hopelessly, boringly, through pain.

But then, if we keep on, we can at last, if we so choose, learn through joy instead.

What a concept!

To learn through joy. This is not the same as happiness, you understand, or satisfaction, or thrill, or excitement, or even contentment. It's not the same as "Have a nice day" or "Let a smile be your umbrella on a rainy day." It's also not about approval or pleasing others or losing twenty pounds (although I wouldn't mind that!). And even though joy, like love, can be found in and through relationships, it's ultimately not about that either.

So what is joy? And where is it? And how do I attain it?

Don't tell me what it's not. Tell me what it is.

Well, there's the old saying "Work is love made visible."

That's a start. For me, my work is joy made visible. Even when I write about sad or uncomfortable or difficult emotions. Work is joy made visible.

Sometimes I think that joy is simplest to find when you cart away the clutter that stands in its way. (There are techniques, in this book and others, that can help you to do just that.) And after you've learned to move energy, train your mind, heal your body, and release your emotions, there will be a lot more room for joy in your life.

Back to joy.

It always comes from the inside. Always. Someone else can share it, but it always comes from within you. Joy's an inside job.

Joy comes out of simplicity. Simplifying your wants, needs, desires. It comes out of balance and order. But not out of giving up. You can still have your dream. You can still fulfill your deepest dream. You can still be your dream. That's joy made manifest.

Joy comes out of health and energy. But not exclusively. I've seen joy at the last of life, as well as at the first.

Sometimes it comes out of peacefulness and rest, after great travail. After witnessing birth or death, it comes. Sometimes it does come out of pain, but mostly it comes after the pain. After the storm has spent itself. After you're still alive no matter what.

Because joy, no matter how corny it may seem, has an awful lot to do with serving others. Joy's a lot like kindness. It multiplies exponentially.

Joy comes when we believe in ourselves. And when we believe in something and someone more than ourselves. When we believe in the divine. When our lives mean something. When we make a difference in the world. That's joy.

But sometimes, we don't recognize joy until after the fact. We know so well what it is *not*, that we're not sure, not certain, if what has touched our lives is really joy. There are so many counterfeits.

But you will know. When joy comes, stealing into your heart, you'll recognize it. You'll know! You'll welcome it.

And ask it back again.

Pity Party

It's amazing the things you learn from friends. Good, solid, loving, caring, long-lasting friends. "Heck-a-mercy!" as they say in Texas, who would have thought that friendships could last so long and mean so much. I have friends all over the world, but I especially have friends in my old hometown on the prairie, friends as durable and sturdy as the pioneer stock they came from.

Because I was gone for seven years and saw the world and experienced a lot and came back changed, you'd think that the old dear friendships of the sixties and seventies and early eighties would have fallen by the wayside, like so much else of the last twenty-five years. But my friendships endured.

Yet there is something we all had to adjust to. I call it *geographical emotions*. In California I learned to express myself, let go, release, get in touch with my anger and other assorted emotions, peel the layers away, and discover who I truly was under culture and conditioning. I learned what I could do and who I was. I soared and plunged and pushed through barriers. But when I had learned the life lessons that

California had to teach me, I came home. To my stoic, sturdy, solid friends. And found acceptance here.

For a while, I had a pity party. You know what that is, don't you? It's about the same as a longtime crying jag, except that you tell your friends about it. I told my friends, those stoic women who also had losses in their lives, losses of loved ones, losses of dreams that now never would come true. Shaking and trembling with all the changes in my life, I leaned on them. You would have thought I was a crazy woman. But my friends did not think so. They steadied me. They saw me through the drama and the trauma. They took me just as I was.

When I could begin to joke about my situation, they laughed with me. You know those levels of laughter, where we mock ourselves while crying underneath? Where common sense tells us we've been down far too long, but emotion still has us by the throat? You know, those pity parties where for a while it's up and down and touch and go, and you realize that a good true friend beats a therapist any day. Of course you know. I had to learn to laugh at myself. I couldn't go on being the tragedy queen, no matter how well I fit the role. I finally had to learn to make light instead of dwelling in the dark.

Well, there came a day when I went into my litany of all my troubles. Again. And my dearest friend in all the world had finally had it. "Don't be a titty baby," she said.

What's a "titty baby"? Seems that in the frontier days, before pacifiers existed, when a baby cried and cried and cried, this is what a mother would do. She'd make sugar water on the stove or else take molasses and dip a clean rag into it and give it to the crying tantrum child. The child would suck on the sweetness and would hush.

My hurts were very real. I had nursed them and nurtured them. I had pity-partied until I was exhausted with myself. I had relied on the sweetness of my nurturing friends to get me through. And now? I was cried out.

"Don't be a titty baby."

Brush yourself off, pick yourself up, go forward, get yourself in order, make a plan, and start all over again.

My friends knew me through and through. They knew I would survive, as I had so many times before. They knew my essential character, the forces that had shaped me, the land I had been born in, and my ancestors, sturdy pioneers all, who pushed forward against far more insurmountable odds than those that had befallen me.

They saw the whole of me, past the pity party and the "titty baby." They did not negate or ignore my pain. They helped me through it and were brave enough to tell me "Enough." They reminded me of who I was, an essential, wise, sturdy woman just like them.

And that's the joy of women's friendships. We hold one another up. We listen and we give advice. We understand each other's grief and loss. But then? But then! We reflect to each other the truth of all we really are, the essential strength and goodness that makes up character.

We say to one another, finally, "Enough. You are more than this."

And that's the strength of women's friendships. To see you through the pity parties, no matter how long it takes. And then to help you make a list. Then to help you see your options. To help you make a plan. Then and only then, to help you up from off your knees and walk with you forward.

That's what friends are for.

The Golden Temple
of the Heart

Here is a simple yet powerful meditation for all those who feel there is not enough love in their lives, whether giving or receiving. It can help you to become a radiant center of love, attracting love to you freely and fully and in turn giving that love freely and fully to all those around you.

Sit quietly relaxed, hands in your lap, palms upward, eyes closed. Take three deep, slow, complete breaths, inhaling and exhaling fully. In these premeditation breaths, the act of proper breathing acts as a sentinel to your body and mind, alerting your deeper self that you are ready for the meditation before you. With each breath, empty out the day and let in clear new possibilities. Then imagine the following scene:

You are walking down a beautiful road that goes up and downhill, winding through hills and valleys, through sunshine and storm. On each side of the road there is beautiful scenery, a pleasant, friendly atmosphere. But you do not stop. You are on your way to a special place.

There! There it is! On the top of that gentle, grass-covered hill. There is a temple, an ancient building set on the hill, in a clearing. The sun glances off its walls. It is venerable, ancient. You feel drawn to the temple, and you go in the open door, into a large vaulted room with a dome open to the sky. There is only one object visible in the large, symmetrical room: an altar with a copper brazier filled with coals. As you draw closer, you see the live coals burst into flame. The flame shoots upward toward the dome of heaven above you. You draw even closer. The flame steadies. You are able to reach out your hands and be warmed by the flame. You contemplate the flame. You feel its warmth, its glow, its light. You reflect on the flowering flame. On the power within a flame, whether candle or bonfire, to warm yourself, to warm the ones you love, to light the way.

You now reach out your hands for your portion of the flame. You are not burned. Instead the flame you cup within your two hands is a loving, glowing warmth for you. You take the flame and gently bring it to your heart. The flame enters the center of your chest. You feel the warmth it generates as part of your own heartbeat. Now both the flame that is within you and the flame still left in the brazier before you in the temple are rising and falling to the rhythm of your breath, to the rhythm of your own heartbeat.

You slowly and reverently walk out of the temple, carrying the flame from the golden temple into the deepest recesses of your own golden temple, your very own heart.

You nourish and cherish the flame within your own heart. You tender its warmth toward others, silently, as you go about your daily work. You feel the red-gold flame beating steadily, lovingly with each beat of your heart, and you realize that this golden temple fire within you cannot be extinguished or depleted.

This continuing stream of fire is always present to warm you. To warm the ones you love, as you extend the flame outward to others. The rhythm of your heartbeat assures and ensures constant inflowing and outflowing of good. The more you tend your flame and tender it to others, the more tenderness you have to give. The more love you give, the more you perceive that love is always there, always available to circulate in your life. You have a golden treasure within you to share with others.

Whenever you feel unloving or unloved, go back to that golden temple and take the fire within you and partake of its eternal love. Each day, see the fire as a rose-gold glow within your heart center. You are a gentle candle. You are a steady flame. You are the golden temple of your heart.

And you are always and forever love.

Replenishing
the
Spirit

TO LISTEN,

TO LEARN,

TO LOVE

MY SOUL

Meditation in Motion

It is six o'clock on a summer morning in Texas. Although the temperature will reach 100 degrees later, at this hour it is cool, quiet, and green. The remnant of a quarter moon hangs in the sky as the sun begins to blossom into view over the nearest line of trees.

What am I doing out at this hour of the morning, walking down a quiet street, the rest of the world just waking up? I am meditating.

I have on thick socks and heavy shoes, and my shorts and cotton top are not designed to show off a middle-aged body to perfection. I am not sitting in a special position, listening to special music, staring at special objects, or repeating special words. Not now. I have done all these things for many years, and I realize the great value in so many methods that can help one through prayer, meditation, and contemplation to move ever closer to the source of being.

But right here and now, moving through space on my own two strong legs, I am meditating. Each breath I breathe is in tune with the morning.

I walk for half a mile, breathing in the morning sounds and fragrances—honeysuckle and hummingbirds. Lights go on; the sounds and smells of breakfast drift from houses. I walk to the school with its flat expanse of grassland awaiting me. Children's voices echo from the early daycare center there. A little red carrot of a boy, all freckles and shining hair, gets out of a car and runs into the school. An elderly man with a considerable paunch, jovial, striding strong, comes into view.

"Good morning. It's six tenths of a mile around on the outside of the fence. I clock it every morning," he tells me earnestly, huffing and puffing as he speaks. A solitary runner—young, bearded, handsome—jogs by, his shoes pounding the concrete.

I am not a concrete person. I begin at the farthest corner of the elementary school playground where, as a little girl, I swung to the sky on the same swings and played baseball on the dirt-packed diamond.

I begin. Smiling, not speaking. It is a solitary commitment. One foot in front of the other. A deep breath. Running!

I am alone now. No one but me in the time and space of here and now. The hard flat slap of the ball and then the heel of the foot on the green and dewy grass, the smell of the earth rising up to meet me, the whish and the swoosh of the wind on my legs, in my hair, the now familiar sensation of my heart and lungs pumping in unison with my legs. I am running!

How many times around the playground? Four? Five? Two miles or three? What are your goals? It used to matter. It used to matter if I could go farther and faster, if I could lose a few pounds and tighten up my stomach muscles. It used to matter if I could win races, or even finish them. It used to matter if I could compete.

It doesn't matter anymore. Now I am running toward God. This is my solitary communion with grass and earth and sky and wind and sun.

For this half hour, or hour, good-bye to goals, good-bye to structure and framework and responsibility. Good-bye negative conditions, situations, emotions. I am meditation in motion. I am stretching my soul with every stride.

Don't push! Don't strain! Throw your heart forward and your feet will follow! When there is no more breath, relax. Slow down. Float in the wind. Rest in the arms of God.

Continue. Visualize. There is a warm and forceful center of energy within. There is unlimited energy within. Release it!

Releasing, releasing. I am releasing now. Good-bye to all cares, all worries, all obstacles, all impediments, all fears.

The rhythm of my breath and the rhythm of my feet are in harmony with the rhythm of my prayers.

And then, when I can go no farther, as the purifying perspiration pours off me, as I slow down to a walk in the sun, I realize cleansing and clearing at the deepest level. Thank you for the blessing of a perfectly functioning physical body.

Then the long, tired, warm walk home. Silent still. Solitary still. A deep, warm, comforting completion within.

Whatever the need for that particular day, whatever lies ahead of me, I realize anew each day that the strength and the joy will flow forth as I need them. God is meeting the need now. As I make that statement, I feel myself flowing into a warm sea of electricity, just flowing with each breath of my being.

Practicing the presence of God takes many forms. There are still many hours of the day waiting to be filled a hundred ways with a hundred prayers. But right now, I am at peace. I am complete, whole, healthful, and joyful, for every day I run toward God.

And God rushes up to meet me, within and without, the sun energy within exploding in rhythm with all that is blessed without.

Every day I run with God. Every day God runs with me, and all is good.

Commanding the Soul

For years I listened to tapes on healing my body, clearing my mind, and opening my heart. Many of them were helpful, and led me, over a period of several years, to a wiser, more loving, healthier, more joyful life. But. There's always a "but" in there somewhere, haven't you noticed? I remember a particular set of tapes that I was very fond of. Whenever I felt stuck or depressed, I would play these tapes and then, determined, go forward to smash through old resistances. I usually felt both stimulated and uplifted by the ideas of unlimitedness presented. But. There it is again.

One of the tapes had a meditation on it wherein after clearing your mind you command your soul to manifest your will. Hmmm. Commanding your soul to manifest your will. I had never heard it put quite that way before. Since I had a strong and passionate will, I had used its dictates for years to get me through crises and obstacles, to get me what I wanted. But I didn't really know all that much about my soul. It was a word that was often used in my meditation books, but I didn't feel that I had a working relationship with my very own soul. I wasn't sure where it was located, if it was located, in my body. Heart? Stomach? Above the crown of my head? Most of the philosophers I studied didn't know that much about it either. So I decided one day that before I would or could command my soul to manifest my will, I needed to find my soul and make friends with it.

I searched for my soul high and low, but having been ignored or differently commanded all these years, it refused to show itself. I used all the tools, techniques, practices, affirmations, and prayers I knew. My soul would not be budged.

I grew disgusted, then frantic. How could I command my soul to manifest my will if it stayed in hiding? Was it a sulky, sullen soul? Was it an indifferent soul? Was it not interested in me and my welfare? Would it turn away from me forever? I kept getting my soul confused with God, my Source, my Creator, and then in the next breath, I searched for my soul among the unresolved issues of my inner child, then within my mind, which had served me so well creatively and logically, and then within my emotions, who made their presence felt through all the peaks and valleys of my reacting self. My soul was not to be found.

I read books on Soul Return and Soul Sacrifice and Soul Retrieval and Spirit and Soul. Nope! Not there! Not high nor low, neither in nor out, not body, not mind, not emotions, not God. Where was my soul and what did it require in order to come forth?

Aha. What did it require? What did it want? I had found a clue. Not in what I wanted from my soul, but instead in asking what my soul wanted from me. Not commanding my soul to manifest my will, but instead, commanding—no, asking—politely, gently, persistently, lovingly. Asking my soul to guide my will. Asking my soul to clear my mind, open my heart, heal my life, replenish my spirit. Asking my soul for help. Asking my guardian angel to lead me to my soul and introduce us.

Gently, in meditation, I sought a sense of my soul's presence. Gently, in meditation, it knocked on the door of my heart center. Knocked from the inside out. For there it stood, deep within my heart, protected, a tightly closed bud waiting for a healing spring to come and nourish it open to flower. Gently it waited for my recognition. I had to give up obstinacy to recognize its presence. I had to reverse my accustomed ways of seeing and feeling and doing in the world in order to be quiet enough to hear my soul's voice. To listen, to learn, to love my soul. To care for my soul.

I no longer command my soul to manifest my will. I honor my soul and I ask it what it requires of me. For its full flowering. For its divine spark within me. For its increasing light. For my soul's work. For my soul's sake.

And my soul answers me and guides me home.

There Are No Monsters Here

This is a story about forgiveness.

One weekend I went to a transformational seminar at a local church. I went to this forgiveness seminar because my co-therapists, a minister and his therapist wife, were sponsoring it. They had been working with me for months on healing my grief.

By the end of two nights and two days, the participants were all exhausted with struggling with their deepest fears and darkest emotions. I was ready to leave. We had had both communion and singing, and I thought, well, that's all there is, I've gotten some good out of this, some relief, but there is still a cold stone of despair lodged in my heart. Will I have to carry it with me my whole life through? Many of the participants had left by then.

But I stayed. I wanted to learn forgiveness once and for all!

The facilitator, an energetic woman in her eighties, asked us to do one last private process. We were to go to separate corners, out-of-the-way hidden places, and search within for one incident, one time when we had failed to forgive ourselves and, by implication, the rest of the world. I did as I was told.

And then something so small, so insignificant, so tiny, so mundane, swam into my consciousness. I remembered a time when my son was dying, and I was taking care of him. I remembered a time in the last six weeks of his life, a night about 3:00 A.M., when, waking from a doze in a chair by the side of his bed, I failed, for one moment in time, to meet his needs, to understand, to be generous, to be unconditionally loving. Just one moment. And this—this—was what stood between me and forgiveness. One moment of time, caught between waking and sleeping, when I, exhausted in mind, body, and emotions, done in, wrung out, prayed out, cried out, burnt out, afraid, anguished, was less than I should have been. It haunted me.

In the forgiveness exercise, we were to identify, face, embrace, and own the situation wherein we had withheld forgiveness from ourselves for much too long. Then we were to offer the situation up in our hands and give it into the hands of the angels. Give it up, release it, erase it, give it over. Then we were to rest and be thankful and be healed.

I did so, and I was.

There are no monsters here.

Those of us who seek forgiveness for errors of omission or commission are simply decent people who have failed to honor and acknowledge our human frailties.

We think that we have failed when all we have really done is to take one more step to learn our life lessons.

It is time and past time to heal the stones of sorrow within our hearts. It is time and past time to forgive ourselves for even the smallest human error, which has loomed so large it has eclipsed our strengths and held us back from joy.

There are no monsters here.

I ask you to forgive.

Spinning My Wheels

Once I decided to try a new spiritual technique that was supposed to heal and balance my chakras and accelerate my growth process. It was a spinning exercise, and I practiced it daily, thirty-three spins at a time, moving just so, breathing and affirming. At the end of thirty days I felt clear and joyful. I took note of the directions once more and discovered that I had been spinning in the wrong direction for thirty days. I had done the exercise backwards! I talked to a healer friend about this process, puzzled and irritated at myself.

She said, "Maybe what you really needed to do, that first thirty days, was to unwind your energy centers, unravel and release all the stored up emotion and energy. Maybe you did it right after all!"

I pondered this. I looked into the mirror. I had been spinning counterclockwise instead of clockwise. I was doing a mirror exercise! In my imagination, I painted a clock on the floor. Slowly and carefully and deliberately, I began to spin in the opposite direction, just as the book instructed. I began laughing. My soul knew what I needed. Joyfully I spun, chanted, breathed, affirmed. Intention is all. I got what I wanted. I reread the book. It said that if I could work up to ninety-nine times a day, I would accelerate into another dimension, even off the planet! I began to laugh again. I decided that I wanted to stay right here, with my feet on the ground, even though my head is in the clouds.

I continue spinning my wheels. Any direction. For as long as I choose.

Decorating My House

I bought an old house that had been built in the twenties. It is situated on an old-fashioned street that looks like a throwback in time to small town life. The house is surrounded by churches—one on each of four close blocks—plus a university founded over a hundred years ago. The church bells begin pealing at eight o'clock every morning. They chime on the hour, until ten o'clock at night. Seven days a week, on the hour, they call me to an instant's joyful prayer. They wake me up in the morning and chime me to bed at night.

My house has a front door made of wood, carved in an arch like a gothic cathedral.

"You need a screen door," my traditional friends exclaim. "You need a standard-size door. You'll never be able to find one that fits."

"No," I say. "I like it the way it is. Bare wood with the rain humming on it, curved like a private cathedral, welcoming me in."

I have wood floors, old and made of pine, while the study and the pantry are asymmetrical flagged stone.

"You need rugs, carpeting, covering," my friends say. "Imagine your heating bills in the winter. You need to decorate. It's so bare."

"No," I say. "I can feel the wood and the stone under my feet, sometimes warm and sometimes cool. I like the way the sun shines in the French doors onto the wood and turns it gold. The cat sleeps in the sunlight there."

"When are you going to put up drapes?" my friends ask me. "For privacy and warmth. When are you going to decorate?"

I have twenty-eight windows and three doors (five, counting the French doors), all uncurtained.

"I like the trees coming in, all that panorama of green," I say. "I like to work at my desk and look out into the sunny street and watch the people go by, young mothers with children, the retired walkers, the university students. I like to sit on my couch with its handmade afghan and let the light pour in from nine windows in one room. I don't want curtains," I say. "I don't want drapes. I like the open space. I like the play of light. I like nature coming in to visit me all day."

"Why don't you clean out your flower beds, trim your branches, cut down your bushes, shape your trees, plant flowers all in a row?" my friends ask me. "Better yet, why don't you move into a condo? Smaller, safer, more reasonable for a single woman."

"I love the leaves falling into my flower beds and covering them for winter, a blanket of colors," I say. "I love the branches of the trees tapping at the window in a friendly way. I love being surrounded on all sides by the wild and green and riotous and still-growing trees and flowers and bushes. I don't want symmetry. I don't want things raked and trained and guided and gutted. I like my wild and overgrown garden just like it is. I don't want a condo. I don't want small rooms and low ceilings, people on top of me and all around me. I want my space of clear green solitude. I am safe. My house surrounds me. My trees protect me. I cherish this house. And it cherishes me."

My friends are finally silent. Until one ventures, "Well, the house looks just like you."

"Thank you," I respond. "It is."

Safe Sex

I am a celibate woman. My gay friends look at me a little uneasily, although they accept me, single and odd as I may be. My straight friends and family venture hopefully, at various intervals, that I would be much happier if I only had a good man to take care of in my life. In my family, the women take care of the men, in large part at least. My family's fondest hope is that "someday he'll come along, and he'll be big and strong," and so on. You know the rest of the song.

I go my own way. For seven years, I worked in the AIDS crisis, and so I am, understandably, reluctant to merge my bodily fluids with anyone, no matter what the conditions or the protection offered. Somehow I've got AIDS and death and sex and intimacy and loss all mixed up together, and it's proved difficult, to say the least, to unwind and unravel each strand that leads from ecstasy to loss.

Like the teachers who naively exhort nubile teenagers in sex education classes to "Just say no," I do. Just say no, I mean. That probably makes me a freak in a society that uses lasciviousness and titillating images to sell everything from cars to deodorant.

Oh, sometimes, in the middle of the night, at three o'clock or so in the morning, I miss a warm body next to mine. It passes.

What I do is go walking.

Usually at dawn, before the street stirs. I'm out with the throw and the slap and the thunk of the morning paper falling on doorsteps. I'm out with the executive joggers, before they face their ties and suits and commutes.

Walking is safe sex for me. You see, you take your deep, sighing breaths and your hair tosses in the wind and you lift your chin a little to gulp in more fresh air, and you close your eyes a little against the warmth of the emerging sun, and your feet and your legs pump in unison and your thighs rub against each other in a rhythm, and you perspire a lot, and your T-shirt and shorts fill with moisture until you could wring them out by the time you've done a mile or so, and you're panting during the second mile, and your joints are growing looser and warmer, and your mind is floating and swaying with the tops of the trees, and everything is, for a few blessed moments, right. Walking as orgasm.

And so I go my way, rejoicing.

Feeding Others

Long ago, when I was a little girl, I used to visit my father's mother, Grandma Cook, in Abilene, Texas. She had a white frame house with a wide stone porch and a japonica tree that dripped brown, shiny pods of litter all over the front yard. It was the backyard that interested me most, though. There where the henhouse and the fenced-off vegetable garden spread across the pasture, even though she was close enough to walk to town, back in those days when it was safe to walk anywhere.

My Grandma was a woman with fine, clear, beautiful skin, which she treated nightly with buttermilk and beaten egg whites so that it would stay that way. Her body was ample and strong and yet squishy in all the right places. She had a lap, not unheard of for Grandmas of that day and age. Her hands, though, were not beautiful, despite the nightly regimen. They were a farm woman's hands, freckled and veined and spotted. They could wring a chicken's neck for Sunday dinner as easy as you please. Strong, raw-boned, useful hands.

I remember standing on a kitchen chair next to the stove when I was seven, helping her to dunk the severed chicken parts first into beaten egg and seasonings, then into flour, then into the hot, sputtering grease in the cast-iron frying pan, that grease saved from rendered bacon fat and used and reused thriftily. None of us knew anything about cholesterol and animal fats then.

So I see myself, an earnest, freckled, "yellow-haired young'un," as my Grandma used to call me, learning at my Grandma's elbow how to cook. I used to watch her hands intently.

I have not thought of her for fifty years.

But I found a poem I had written in what I call my struggling days, that time when I was trapped and frantic in my life, and discontent and bewilderment seeped into the corners of the house where I lived. And into the lives of the men I fed. The times, they were a-changin', but in Texas small towns, everything and everyone remained the same. Like my Grandma, I fed men, both constantly and interminably, or so it seemed to me at the time.

Later, much later, the poem I wrote in the sixties won a prize and was published, and I was triumphant because I had turned straw into gold. I had, by some mysterious alchemy, combined past memories with present discontent. I invented a Grandma who yearned for more. I had so much of it to spare.

Now, past my rebellious years, past the years of feeding men (she had three sons, I had four), I remember her life as being just right for her, after all. Maybe there were days of yearning, nights of despair. It happens a lot, in every woman's life I know. But she kept on, through husband and sons dying, through all the mishaps and disappointments that women are prey to.

She fed other people, both male and female. She fed me. When did I decide that her gift to others was nothing more than a demeaning task? Surely it is nurturing and loving and kind to feed others. Why couldn't I see past the beaten biscuits, past the jeweled jars of home-canned peaches and pickles, past the laden table at the family Sunday dinner?

She fed her soul when she fed us. She fed our souls too.

My Grandma lived until her late eighties, and when she died she still had that beautiful, translucent, papery-thin but barely wrinkled skin. And her hands stayed strong.

Come Home

When someone we love dies, our grief is for the living. The soul released from the body soars onward, going home. For sometimes death is a kind friend; release from pain, release into the all-embracing light, is a reward, not a punishment. For those of us left behind, grieving on the shore, I offer this passage. It expresses what I believe may be awaiting our loved one on the other side:

COME HOME

Come home.
The tower waits.
The sea is still.
Dark gone. Light breaks.
Do what you will.

Serene, the tower.
Serene, the waiting sea.
Come home
Alone
Wherever you may be.

The hour creates the hour.
I come to tell you.
Only
Come home
To filling sea,
To towers that will not fall.
To infinity.
I come to tell you of that energy.

And of that high and holy power within
Your own serene and inner citadel.
Come home.

We too can come home when our loved one dies. We can come home to a luminous acceptance of the truth about the light. We can let the light embrace us and sustain us. We can come home to our own faith, our own courage, our own light that shines within, without, and all around us as we move forward, released from pain as our loved one has been released, awaiting reunion and renewal, awaiting our own homecoming.

Hoarding Expected Grief

Sometimes we have to go through crises of such magnitude, such violent, unexpected change, changes that carry so many responsibilities, so many sacrifices (or so we perceive), so many lessons to be learned, that sometimes, to keep ourselves from exploding, from falling apart, from dissolving, from dying, sometimes we hoard. We hoard our pain. We swallow our rage. We conceal our resentments. We bury guilt, false guilt—it is almost always false guilt. We have done the things we ought not to have done. We have made mistakes along this trail of tears. We have railed at God and turned away to cover our wounds. We have disappeared from life. We have opted out. We have allowed ourselves to fail and fail again. Or so we perceive when we examine our faults and our shortcomings and our victimization. So we perceive.

Afterwards, putting on our smiley faces, putting on our masks, clothing ourselves in acceptable personas, armoring ourselves against more blows, more disappointments, we go forth. And no one knows. Or so we think. But our bodies say otherwise. We clothe ourselves in haunted, hollow-eyed rigidity, or, as is more often the case, we clothe ourselves in impervious substantial bodies. We throw a life preserver around us to hold our feelings in.

We hoard. As we hoard our money against another rainy day. For there have been so many, and it looks like there will be many more. Surely there will not be enough to get us through them all.

So we go this far and no further. We crawl away into our beds to renew, to fill up, to be made whole. We hoard our energies. We hoard our talents, abilities, ideas. We often hoard our love. When we feel unloved, we often hoard the little we have left. We become grudging givers, if we can give at all.

In the dark night of the soul, we hoard our grief. Expressed and unexpressed, an ocean of grief, never ceasing, continues through us, and we clasp it to us. After all, it is all we have left.

We hoard our pain. Letting it out into the light of day hesitantly, rarely, peeking over our shoulders to see if it's all right to do so, venting ourselves in anger rather than saying out loud "I hurt, I grieve." Telling everyone that we are all right, we are over it, it's okay, no need to worry, after all tomorrow is another day and we will be all right tomorrow, if tomorrow ever comes. We hoard our grief. It lies inside us like a stone.

Time passes. Sometimes we heal a little or a lot, but never fully. We function. We survive. But what about our grief? Pushed down, stifled, denied, buried. Forgotten. Another crisis comes. Another loved one is ill. Someone else dies, and someone else. Love walks away from us. The places where we once flourished fall into ruin. Our dreams die too. Our energies are concentrated on functioning and surviving, not in allowing, not in creating, not in flowing forth. Sometimes we decide to deny that part of us that still hurts, that unhealed, unloved, despairing part of us that we have forgotten, that part of us we never give the time of day to, that undernourished part of us. We decide that it does not exist.

Then that part of us decides that grief is all it has, that pain is its province, that light and love and healing have passed it by. It adjusts. It accommodates. It hides. Sometimes it even anticipates. Then our grief, no matter how kind we have been to it, no matter if we have honored its presence and allowed its mourning—and most of us do not—or only let it out a little, because it hurts too much, sometimes then our grief expects and welcomes more. It decides to hoard itself and multiply and hold fast and even anticipate more and more of the same. Our grief prepares for more. We hoard expected grief.

How do we heal this expected, anticipated, past, present, future, grief? We let it out. Hesitantly, privately, sometimes with a friend, sometimes with professional help, sometimes with prayer. We let it out little by little, through movement and work and thoughtful recognition. We let it run its course. It can overwhelm us then, this grief so long unexpressed or expressed only partly. Sometimes we feel as though we are merely a skin filled with tears.

But we are more. When energy is allowed—even encouraged—to flow, then so it does, moving out from its hiding place, waiting to be recognized, waiting to be acknowledged, expressed, paid attention to, honored, respected. And it won't go back into its box of body. It can't! It must run its course. No matter if we or others disapprove. It must come into the light. It must be given forth, given up, given away. Free flow, free fall, loosed to the light, released and healed. But it must not be hoarded. Let it out! Let it dissipate. Let it disappear. Let it be transformed. Let it go. Hoard no more. Let tomorrow come in joy. Begin again. Begin now.

Fear Forward

"Whenever I'm afraid or weary of responsibilities or searching to find my way, I use the words *fear forward* as a talisman to light me through the dark. It is a way of telling myself that I am here in this body to confront my fears and move through them, not to run away, not to dwell on the fears and stay with them or wallow in them, but to go through them and past them, like a laser beam of light that takes the unbearable feelings in me and transforms them into action."

I first wrote those words in 1985, when I had just discovered that my dear son Michael had AIDS. Our journey together, through his and my dark night of the soul and eventual release into the light, was both agony and luminescence. Much of what I have learned about courage and unconditional love came from the two years we had together before he left the world.

My fear had nothing to do with catching a dread disease. It had to do, instead, with learning my own depths, my own strengths. I was afraid that I would fail him. I was afraid that I could not be strong enough, wise enough, loving enough, brave enough to journey with him through his most intense challenge.

Later, I turned grief into action. I worked for seven years in the AIDS crisis, writing, lecturing, publishing. This changed my life. When the seven years were done, I left that life and came home to heal.

I found then that we are what we have done, we are our experiences, our sorrows, our rage, our fears. Especially our fears.

Part of my own Soulwork has been to reconcile weakness with strength, illness with health, safety with risk, expansion with contraction, and the age-old themes of life and death and loving and giving with the need for acceptance and receiving. These are not just words on a page. They are the central issues, the central struggles, if you will, of my life. Are these your issues too?

What if we all decided that we would "fear forward" into our own psyches, into our own deepest, hidden, ignored, denigrated anguish of the soul? That we would take a spiritual journey to see who we are, what we are made of, what we are worth? This is a perilous journey indeed, to look within at all we have denied ourselves, all we have ignored in the name of others' needs, wants, wishes, and desires. It is a "fear forward" that has little sanction in society, scant understanding or approval from others. It is a commitment to self that garners no laurels from the outside world. Cannot we be both strong and weak? Both caregiver and care-receiver? Both courageous and at times terrified?

"Fear forward" I say to myself when I begin to probe my dreams or write a book or take the next step forward in healing my life. "Fear forward" I say when there seems to be no sustenance for me, no recognition of my true soul. We must give that recognition, that respect, that sustenance to ourselves. We must discover our own worth and courage. We must be as true and loving and honoring to ourselves as we have been to others. This is not selfishness, no matter what the world says to us. This is commonsense courage. This is "fearing forward" for ourselves.

Then and only then can we can fly forward, streaming energy, wisdom, love, goodwill, and a fierce recklessness born of discovering, acknowledging, owning, and releasing our own deepest fears. Discovering, acknowledging, owning, and receiving our own true self.

Finding the Center

"I turn within to the limitless resources of Spirit, and I am filled with light, wisdom, and peace."

Again and again, many of us have murmured the words of this self-searching, soul-searching prayer. Again and again, we have asked the questions: "How do I get soul-centered? How do I get to God?"

The avenue exists in the single word "Listen"!

Ask, yes. Ask again and again. But after the asking comes the listening. Just listen.

And as the listening begins, we need not be overly concerned with what may appear at first to be a total, all-absorbing preoccupation with the self—the "selfish" self as we may have been conditioned to think of it. Instead, we should acknowledge, recognize, uncover, love, and trust that self—that uniqueness that is our outer nature.

What then? After the self-searching, the self-finding, the self-awareness, we are ready for much more.

We are ready to let the soul-self predominate—that self

which is in and around every cell of the body, centered within as a manifestation of our own highest and best self. We are ready to trust, to listen to this God-self, this God-power within. This is the light we have been searching for. This is the energy. This is the love. This is the spark of God within each of us that can be fanned into a roaring flame. This is the fire from heaven.

When we allow the flowing forth of that divine force, our lives will be transformed because we have been transformed. Crises may come, tests and sorrows may appear, but we will be different. Each crisis then will be an opportunity for spiritual growth, each test an avenue for unfolding spiritual good in our lives. It may take much prayer, but the light is always there. The light is our life. We are the light within.

To be soul-centered then is to lay down the heaviness, the thickness, the thicket of problems that surround us. To let go of everything and everyone. To bless and to release people, conditions, situations, attitudes, emotions. To let the light shine. To trust in God. To uncover and recover the soul-force within.

To be soul-centered is to work from the center, in a calm knowing, in a calm believing, in a calm acceptance of others, of ourselves, of life. Of God. Then we are truly inner-directed. Then we are truly practicing the presence of God in our lives.

Love and trust the soul within you. It is your limitless resource. It is light, wisdom, and peace.

Listen! It is God in action in your life.

Green and Silver Tree Woman

There is an ancient silver-leaf maple that I can see from my window as I write. It has been in the neighborhood for about one hundred and fifty years, long before the houses and the people came. It is a beautiful tree, lush, full, green most of the year. It gives shade to the whole street, and the birds and the squirrels use its branches for their home. It is rooted solidly, fully, its source deep in the earth underneath the sidewalks.

This green tree is a symbol of energy and renewing life for me. I greet it every morning and every night. Sometimes it seems to answer back to me, with a salute from its leafy branches. It follows the seasons as I do, from its first sweet greening in the spring, to its full-bodied sunlit leaves in the summer heat, to its riot of gold and orange and brown leaves lifting and falling in the autumn, to its stripped and silvery branches leaning upward to the winter sky. Then, as always, spring comes again and my green tree, my good-morning tree, comes alive once more in a profusion of new leaves.

Beneath the ancient tree, right across the street, there is a new silver-leaf maple, planted only last year. It too is tended lovingly and faithfully, watered and staked so that it will survive the heat of the Texas summer and the "blue northers" that come down from the prairie in the spring.

The ancient tree leans protectively over the young tree, providing it with cooling shade and (I like to think) offering reassurance to the new young tree so that it too can grow to its own majestic height, to its own fullness and ripening.

To me, the process of aging is the process of growing from a new, green, somewhat shaky tree to the flowering of the ancient, eternal verities symbolized in the aged tree. The mature tree offers wisdom and solace. It protects, it buffers, it shades, it shields, it nurtures and nourishes. I like to think that I will age as gracefully and as naturally as my good-morning tree. For it does not seek to be anything other than what it is. It has already experienced countless springs, summers, autumns, and winters. It endures. It flourishes. It is a joyful, renewing source. It honors nature as it honors itself. It shines with its own splendor.

In *Childhood and Society* psychologist Erik Erikson set forth a theory called the "Eight Stages of Man." In it, he says that the aging stage, the maturing stage of one's life, will be one wherein we choose either "integrity or disgust." I have never forgotten those words.

The alternative to aging is leaving the planet. But as we do age, as we do move from green shoot to ancient nurturer, we choose again and again. Daily we choose. Complaining or courage. Dependency or interdependency. Resentment or acceptance. Creator or destroyer. Integrity or disgust.

It's time for you to choose. Which do you choose, green-tree, silver-branched, good-morning woman?

Angels and Archangels

Angels are hot stuff this year. Book after book. There's even an angel industry. As they say in Hollywood about a popular movie that reaches a lot of people, "It's got legs." Well, the prevailing theory about angels is not that they have legs (who knows?), but that they are all around us, just waiting and hoping that we will notice them. I'm ready. I'm waiting and hoping too.

When I was a little girl there was a bedtime prayer I used to say. Something about "Matthew, Mark, Luke, and John, bless the bed that I lie on." And then, of course, you just knew that all four bedposts were guarded by ancient, supernatural beings and that you would be safe all night long.

Lately there have been a rash of angel sightings. For those of us who find the idea of God somewhat daunting, the idea of a guardian angel is more personal, more comforting, more accessible somehow, closer to home. I'm sure I have one. Don't you?

I've been studying angels. And sometimes I call upon them. There are four archangels, or so I've read. Of course there are countless angels, but the archangels have been named and numbered in ancient and modern texts.

The four archangels that watch over us and all the world are Michael, Gabriel, Rafael, and Uriel. (In some books, the spellings change.) And there is a blissful meditation in which you can surround yourself with these powerful archangels. Michael, who symbolizes unconditional love, is on your right side; Gabriel, who helps you to heal all your fears, is on your left side; Uriel, the angel of clear perception and clear seeing, who goes before you and opens the door to understanding and good, is in front of you, leading the way; and then there is Rafael, who stands behind you in comfort, healing, and protection.

Sometimes I almost think I see them, out of the corner of my eye, but when I shift my gaze, they are gone.

But my guardian angel, my very own special comforter and guide, is always here for me. I know this with deep conviction, even as I know my name.

I may joke about the other angels. I may be in awe at even the possibility of archangels. I may call upon them and wonder, always wonder if they hear me, if they care. I may fall asleep easily and gently, with the blissful hope of being surrounded by celestial beings. But I'm not totally sure of those impersonal, huge beings that oversee the world. I tend to think, most days when I turn on the evening news, that we have need of thousands, even millions, of wise and powerful angels to heal the world.

Some people talk about our better angels. Is this the better part of us? Or is it just a phrase, just a phase we go through on our way to spiritual understanding? Some people say that by performing both personal and random acts of kindness we may entertain angels unaware. I like to think that's so. Some people say that angels rush in, fools in the way or not, whenever they are needed. I like to think that's so too.

I am no expert on angels. But I have the sense, more and more, day by day and night by gentle night, that they are all around, with their nurturing wings and their kind eyes, watching, listening, helping.

My guardian angel tells me that it's true.

Integration of
the Four Bodies

Sometimes it feels to me that my mind is in one place, my emotions are in another, my body is running along trying frantically to catch up, and my spirit is out to lunch.

That's when I get up an hour early and take the time to do a powerful integrative meditation called, appropriately enough, *Integration of the Four Bodies*.

This practice is not as esoteric as it may seem. To those of you who have barely dipped a toe into the water of the unconscious, this meditation will make a believer out of you. Its purpose is simply to unite and integrate the four aspects of your being: the physical, the mental, the emotional, and the spiritual.

So here goes:

Find a quiet place, free from interruptions, and either sit in a chair with your spine straight, your feet planted firmly on the floor, and your hands loosely held, palms open to receive, in front of you, or sit cross-legged (or, if you are more flexible, in a half-lotus Yoga position), open hands resting on your thighs.

If you are tired or ill, you can lie down instead. But sitting erect in this basic meditative posture allows energy to flow freely up and down your spine.

Now begin to take slow deep breaths from the very center of your being and begin to visualize light pouring down from on high, first covering your body with light and breath and then allowing the light to move down and into each of the seven wheels of light within your body, the seven chakras. Pour the light down through and over the crown of your head, the center of your forehead, your throat, your heart center in the middle of your chest, your third chakra in your midsection, your second chakra center between your navel and your pubic bone, and the root chakra at the base of your spine. Pour the light through and onward and downward until you pour the light through your feet and down through the floor and into the ground and into the earth. This grounds you and anchors the light. This in itself is a basic meditation to move energy, balance and energize your chakras, and ground you so that your work reflects your spiritual energy made manifest. But this is only the first part of the meditation.

When you feel grounded, balanced, and filled with light, begin to contact and call forth the four aspects of your being: the physical body, the mental body, the emotional body, and the spiritual body. Ask them to come forth in a room inside your heart that you have set up for them. You can put a conference table there in your heart, if you so choose. I like to use the heart center because it helps to work through the heart with all you do. You can give a color, a shape, a form, to each of the four bodies. They are all you, and they are waiting to be called on.

Now talk to the four bodies assembled in your heart. Ask them for their advice, their input, on whatever task or healing or responsibility is facing you. You can say something like "Well, it seems like we are not pulling together" or "I feel fragmented, like some of you are on vacation" or "Please help me to understand what's going on."

Ask the four bodies what they need from you and from each other in order to be unified and whole. Ask them to cooperate. Ask them to blend their energies in harmony for the sake of the whole you, for the sake of the soul of you. Engage them in dialogue. Ask for deep insights, true healing, revealing guidance. They will not disappoint you.

Sometimes you may find that your mind is so far ahead of your physical body that the body is just waiting to reel you in, to slow you down, to say "Notice me! I need rest and less stress." Sometimes you may find that the emotional body is still wrestling with an old hurt that it has tried to transfer to the physical body, where it hopes it will be noticed. Sometimes you may find that the mental body is tired of all its planning and just wants to let the physical or the spiritual body take over. So ask now. Then listen to the answers from each of the four aspects of your being.

Each time you do this meditation, you will find clues to how you truly operate at the deepest and highest levels of your being. For you are more than flesh and bone. You are more than your emotions. You are more than mental exercises. You are even more than your spiritual self, for you are four bodies in one, and whenever any one of your four bodies is unbalanced they will let you know.

Sometimes when I have a challenging task before me I call upon my four bodies to unite in prayer with me, hands clasped, all colors blending, merging, working with me, not against me. I ask for harmony within the physical, mental, emotional, and spiritual aspects of my being. I am never disappointed. Often startling revelations come to me, gifts from spirit, mind, emotions that help to bless and heal my body temple. Often, if I listen closely, the different aspects of my being will ask for help and cooperation from each other. This seems a mystical process, it is true, but it is a practical one as well. Why not use all of you, cooperating wisely and lovingly together, in every task that faces you? Why not ask for guidance, help, healing, inspiration, kindness, energy from all of you? Then you may be more unified, more whole.

To end this meditation, simply thank each of your four bodies and release them to their tasks. Sit quietly for a moment in the energy. Then breathe your way back up to the everyday world. Stretch and move and breathe deeply.

And go your way rejoicing.

Grandmother Vision

I went to my very first Native American drumming ceremony the other night. Eight women of varying ages gathered in a space to drum and chant and sing and express their truths. They brought food too. Oh my! What a blessing that night was!

·I had studied and read and practiced my spiritual path for years, but I had never, until this night, experienced rituals based on Native American traditions.

Our leader for the evening, a young woman with an old soul, a teacher and midwife, an explorer of new paths, shared with us what she had learned, in a circle of women placed just so, with our drums and rattles at the ready. She told us about women coming together at the waxing and the waning of the moon, and the correlated menstrual cycles that accompany this moon time, and the wisdom of midwifery, and the ways of Grandmother Moon.

Grandmother Moon! My ears pricked up at that. I knew of course the stages of a woman's life —child, maiden, mother, crone—and had learned to celebrate inside just where I was in the varied cycles of a woman's life.

But this woman told us more. She told us that it is Grandmother Moon, the elder woman of the tribe, who holds the courage, the wisdom, the vision. From her deep soul we are nourished. She talked about Grandmother Moon, and Grandmother Courage, and Grandmother Warrior, and Grandmother Wisdom, and Grandmother Visionary.

We began to beat our drums. We began to sing songs of wisdom. The stones we had gathered from river and stream bed and ocean, from mountain and prairie, glowed before us. We began to chant. Energy lifted and circled.

All of the other women at the ceremony were younger than myself. They still bled. They still gave birth. They still raised children and looked for love in many places. Their lives were ahead of them. They had learned, far earlier than I, the mystery and the blessing of women in touch with their bodies. How I wish that I had learned in earlier years what they so confidently knew already. But. I could be Grandmother Moon. Grandmother Courage. Grandmother Warrior. Grandmother Wisdom. Grandmother Visionary. This I could grab hold of, breathe in, incorporate within my very soul.

We turned to our stones. Why is it that stones, when used in ritual, hold so much power? We placed our individual, lovingly gathered stones precisely on our bellies. We wanted to heal and bless that feminine force within.

I remembered a novel I once wrote that had as its theme the generational teachings of one woman to another and that carried, as its symbol, an amulet given in the desert to the heroine, an amulet shaped like and called a womb-stone. Its power and its teachings had been passed down from one wise woman to another, in a family chain.

I put my treasured stone upon my empty, surgically excised womb. But I was full. I knew my task.

Sometimes it only takes a word, a phrase, a drumbeat, a circle, a song, a room full of women in harmony together, to remind us of all that we are.

Grandmother Moon, Grandmother Courage, Grand-mother Warrior, Grandmother Wisdom, Grandmother Vision. I chanted the names of myself to myself silently. And felt my body, my Grandmother body, fill with power and quiet joy.

Reversing the Energy

You never know when messages will fall into your lap at the exact instant you need them. The key is recognizing the messages when they appear. Here is one exercise I found that worked for me. I call it "Reversing the Energy."

As spiritual beings encased in human bodies, it is our nature to fill our bodies with all the emotions and shocks of life that we cannot handle at the time they happen. Unless you are a wild woman who can afford the luxury of instant screaming, shouting, crying, releasing, and processing at the exact moment of each emotional blow (and they would cart you off to an asylum if you did just that!), there's bound to be an immense amount of feeling, plus your conclusions about those feelings, stuck in various places in the temple of your body. Like a chrysalis encased in a protective cocoon.

Now, I'm not talking here about simplistic Metaphysics 101, where there is an exact symptom to correspond to an exact thought and any symptom of ill health at all means that you are spiritually lacking—of course, if you weren't, your life and your body would work perfectly. To me, these judgments are every bit as heinous, sometimes erroneous, and one-sided as a traditional health professional diagnosing a terminal disease with dire pronouncements, no hope, and only invasive treatments or drugs to treat it. Sometimes they're wrong and sometimes they're right and sometimes they're both half-right and half-wrong—and what does diagnosis have to do with healing your pain anyway?

Just as in your dreams, when it is far wiser to find your own symbols, your own personal way of managing your complicated unconscious, rather than consulting a dream dictionary, so too when doing Soulwork, you may find your life written on your body, but in a multi-layered, multi-dimensional, multi-faceted way. In other words, a pain in the gut may mean indigestion or cancer, or a damaged digestive system, or even unassimilated trauma. It's what you do with the information that counts. Sometimes contemplating your navel is useful after all!

For a multitude of reasons, there may be pain in your body and pain in your life. Here is what you can do, whatever your belief system about healing may be. You can take your hand and place it on that part of your body, especially where there is chronic discomfort or bodily damage. And then ask, gently and lovingly and with your eyes closed and your heart open, for stuck, enclosed, encased, buried energy to be released from your body (where it can no longer be contained properly) and dissipated instead into the atmosphere. It's best to do this thoughtfully and willingly and privately and to allow time for the emotion to come forth. Don't stop the emotion when it comes. For it surely will. Like an avalanche. So be prepared. And be willing to have it so. You want the buried energy that causes pain in the body to be released out of the body and reversed—so that the energy once used to bury emotional pain in a bone or joint or organ or gland can now be freed.

The old saying that depression is anger turned inward is a good example here. You free the energy from the body, where it may have caused chronic discomfort, and you talk to your pain, you ask it for its truth, you ask it what it wants, you listen to your pain, you own it and honor it and release it and change it into something different. Fuel for the soul. Reversed energy.

The next few days of your life will be fireworks. Be prepared—a shift will occur. For our bodies were never meant to contain the enormous unspoken, unacknowledged, unexpressed feelings of a lifetime. By reversing the energy, we free ourselves of emotional burdens and long-held pain. We change the energy into another form. Then can it be poured out into the world as creation instead of inward, insidious destruction. We become shape-shifters with the energy. We use it instead of allowing it to use us. Isn't that what transformation is?

Soulwork is more than changing thought forms. Soulwork is about changing emotional energies as well, requiring courage and creativity and curiosity and willingness and trust. Soulwork is the act of transformation itself. It frees you to be whole.

But you have to reverse the energy first.

When I Am an Old Woman

When I am an old woman, I shall wear green and yellow and red and blue, bold primary colors that tell the world that I am coming. Colors of light and energy. When I am an old woman, I will dab on cinnamon perfume and dance with my grandchildren at family weddings and hug fat cousins at family funerals and only wear dresses on special occasions. I will throw away my panty hose like I threw away my high heels, and I will wear loose comfortable clothes with interesting textures that sweep around my ankles on cold winter nights.

I will have a cat, a female Siamese, and it will be both mellow and independent, like me. It will not suffer fools gladly, nor converse in any way with idiots. Nor will I.

When I am an old woman, I will read all night if I so choose, and when sleep still eludes me I will go out to the backyard in the middle of the night, being careful to put on my robe and spectacles, and I will whisper songs of my own making to the full moon, while my cat curls around my ankles. And the moon may answer me. When I am an old woman.

When I am an old woman, I shall refuse to lie, although I must admit, fibs are useful for kindness. And I mean to be kind.

When I am an old woman, I shall laugh hysterically with other old women, as we help each other across the street. I shall bring casseroles for company if asked, but otherwise I shall live alone in a house with an overgrown garden and commit my life to paper and sing lullaby songs my own old woman grandmother sang to me.

When I am an old woman, I will do exactly as I please. I will get up when I please and go to bed when I please and eat when and what I please, because life's too short for rules and regulations anymore, and anyway old women are invisible and so can do exactly as they please.

So this is what I will do, when I am an old woman. I will not go out on rainy afternoons. Instead, I will sit in my wide, warm, green and yellow cottony armchair by the fire, with my independent, mellow cat like an afghan on my lap. I will sprinkle herbs into my tea and suck the honey off the stirring spoon. My cat and I will purr and dream, while the winter wind knocks at the windowpane. I will remember then all the loves of my life and some who never loved me at all, but it is of no matter to me now. I will remember all the bright days and dark nights of my life, like a rosary slipping across my forehead, I will remember.

And I will hold no regrets. I will be satisfied. When I am an old woman.

I'm starting now.

Drawing Down the Light

I'm almost always looking for the light. I already did the dark night of the soul. It took me seven years. Maybe closer to ten. I had to learn both dark and light, both death and life. So now I'm almost always looking for the light. I reflect on it daily. Does it reflect in me? Could be. I have high hopes.

In meditation, I learned to draw down the light, draw it down from some great cistern in the sky, pour it over my head and down my body, pour it through me as well, through every chakra, through every organ, gland, and muscle, through blood and bone.

"Make your mind a lighted lamp," a teacher once told me. I think of the old-fashioned brass and glass lamps my grandmother had, with elaborate, tasseled fabric shades. You would pull on a tassel to turn on the light, and it would flow through the shade, making an intricate pattern. I pull on the tassel of my lamp. I am then within the soft illumination within the shade. I am not the lampshade. I am the lighted lamp.

"Lead, Kindly Light," my forefathers and foremothers used to sing in church. I have a friend who is a "Lead, Kindly Light" person. Solid, warm, wise, comforting, kind. I have seen other people's lights as well. One a trembly candle in the wind, buffeted by chance and circumstance; one a blaze of colored, twinkling Christmas lights; one all luminescence before his light went out. There are hard-edged fluorescence, lean, high-tech lights, conserving energy. There are sunlight and moonlight and floodlight and flashlight people.

Sometimes I go outside and sit on my terrace steps whenever there is winter sunshine and I lift my face to the weak rays of winter and I let the sunlight, however tentative it may be, pour through my forehead. I was told once that if you lift your uncovered forehead to the sunlight for fifteen minutes every day, your pituitary, the master gland between your eyes, in back of the pineal gland, in back of what is known in meditation as the third-eye point, will open to the sun and rev itself up and keep you healthy. I try it often. It feels like a warm hand on my forehead, a gentle tickly bee walking across the promontory between my eyes. Surely you can spare fifteen minutes, eyes closed, to contemplate the light? To let the light in. To brighten the corner where you are? To let your light shine?

I used to think that a laser-like beam of concentration was required to make things happen. I have often used that one-pointedness to create. But lately, I've been reading quantum physics. And there is a phrase that haunts me like a poem. It is this: "Light can be both wave and particle." It's like a mantra, an affirmation, a humming sound that slides off the tongue in liquid light. Light can be both wave and particle. Light undulates like a wave as it comes to strike the retina of the eye and reverses the picture so that we can see light. More and more light. As the light comes in and as it goes forth, it translates images. I have oversimplified, but you get the picture. It's like when you see light shimmering in front of you on long car trips on desert highways, that tantalizing mirage in front of you that looks like waves of light or waves of water. Just out of reach.

Light can be both wave and particle, so that when you visualize something, anything that you want to happen, when you cast your dream out in front of you and ask that it not only reach its destination but come back to you bearing gifts, it does so in waves of light. Not headlights, not glare. For light is wave.

And I am told that light is also particle. In fact, we are each filled with myriad winking, blinking, minute, on and off, coming and going, arranging and rearranging, swarming bee lights inside of us.

So yes, things can be changed, healing can occur, thought can be rearranged, emotion can be transformed into motion itself, the motion of the light, both wave and particle.

And so I immerse myself in light, in the daytime so that words and ideas and feeling and healing and love can occur, and at night, because don't you think you really need light to guide you through your dreams and protect and nourish your sleeping body as well?

So I draw down the light and I anchor it down through my feet and into the earth—it helps if you stand outside for this, at dawn, and let your feet touch solid earth and let light penetrate down to the center of the earth—in fantasy—and draw the light in and down and up and all around so you are surrounded by a bubble of light.

That's one way.

It's good to do at sunset too. And at night. Just draw the wave of light up over you like a blanket. Use any color you choose. Gold is best for me, with tinges here and there of blue. You'll know.

Then you are not only nourished, guided, and protected by the light, you are the light itself. In every cell, in every pore, you are light. You are both wave and particle.

Then nothing is impossible.

Twelve Directions for Soulwork Living

1. Begin to think of yourself as a spiritual being encased in a human body, instead of a human being with a lost or forgotten soul.

2. Honor the temple of your body by treating it with courtesy and kindness, and filling it with healthy food and pure water. Clear your body of whatever poisons, toxins, and stimulants you may have choked it with for years. Search out the nutrition, the herbs, and the natural remedies that can help you on this quest. Move your body, whatever its age and condition. Go toward health, not atrophy.

3. Create a nurturing environment for yourself. Whether you're in a one-room apartment or a mansion, whether you work outdoors in nature or in a stressful situation, throw out the ugliness and begin to create beauty in your life. A coat of paint or a vase of flowers adds color, light, warmth, and space and creates a safe haven. Whatever your soul longs for, begin to create it now. Beauty multiplies.

4. Spend some time alone each day to replenish your soul. Whether it's a walk in the park or a formal meditation spot or a sacred space you have created for yourself, spend some time alone, wherever and however you can. Get to know yourself gently and quietly without noise or chatter or TV or freeways.

5. Clear your mind of toxic thoughts. Search out your core beliefs about yourself and the world. Clear your mind of blame. A caring therapist can help. Fast from victimhood. Feast on clarity.

6. Honor your emotions and be willing to work through resentments, fears, worries, guilt, and grief. This is an ongoing process that gets easier as you release years of hurt and anger. Be gentle with yourself. Ask for help as you need it. Emotions are neither negative nor positive in themselves; they are an expression of your deepest feelings. Face, embrace, release, erase.

7.   Love and accept yourself, no matter what it takes to come to that love. Love your body, mind, emotions, and spirit, whether they fit an ideal or not. Love your unique self. Love where you are now in your life and where you have been and where you are going. *Then* love and accept others. This is the second part of the process. One seldom works without the other. You begin by forgiving everyone and every experience in your life that has brought you to this day. Forgive yourself. Forgive fate and circumstances. Forgive God. Continue the process daily.

8.   Find something or someone to believe in. God, Jesus Christ, Buddha, a higher power, angels, the Great Mother, the divine. This belief may or may not require attendance at a church or synagogue or temple. But attend to that spiritual part of your life daily, as best you can, whether in prayer or meditation, meeting with others or alone. Deepen your spiritual life.

9. Work with passion. Find something that moves you and practice and learn and study and perfect your craft. Refuse to measure your worth by a paycheck. Serve the world with your work.

10. Be willing to grow, to learn, to start over. Be flexible. Everything in life is change. There are no failures, just experiences. Be curious about life. Never stop learning. See yourself at the end of your life, active, vital, wise, creative, compassionate. Go toward that goal with zest and enthusiasm.

11. Give. Give to others. Give to yourself. Give to the environment. Give to your families. Give to your friends. Give with your work, your time, your energy, and whatever support seems to be called for. Never be afraid to give. What you give comes back to you tenfold. And if by chance you do not feel this in your life and soul at this time, do it anyway. Watch the results.

12.   Receive. Learn from everything and everyone in your world. Allow others to give to you as well. Receive the gifts of the spirit in your prayer and meditation. Receive the gifts of joy and companionship. Receive the gift of a job well done. Receive the gift of books that teach and entertain and inspire. Receive the gift of breath, of life, of moving your body and your mind and your emotions and your spirit. Receive the gift of love. Accept the gifts as they are offered, without judgment. Open your hands, your heart, your soul to receive. Then comes Grace.

About the Author

BettyClare Moffatt, M.A., is a prominent
writer and public speaker in the fields
of AIDS, death and dying, grief recovery,
and women's spirituality. She is the author
of *When Someone You Love Has AIDS* and
several other books. She divides her time
between Texas, New Mexico, and California.

Wildcat Canyon Press and New World Library
are dedicated to publishing books and audio
cassettes that help improve the quality
of our lives. For a catalog of our fine
books and audio cassettes, contact:

Wildcat Canyon Press
New World Library
14 Pamaron Way
Novato, CA 94949
Phone: (415) 884–2100
Fax: (415) 884–2199

Or call toll free:
(800) 227–3900